Young Children's Creative Thinking

D0530961

REEF

Education at SAGE

SAGE is a leading international publisher of journals, books, and electronic media for academic, educational, and professional markets.

Our education publishing includes:

- accessible and comprehensive texts for aspiring education professionals and practitioners looking to further their careers through continuing professional development

- inspirational advice and guidance for the classroom

- authoritative state of the art reference from the leading authors in the field

Find out more at: **www.sagepub.co.uk/education**

Young Children's Creative Thinking

Hiroko Fumoto, Sue Robson,
Sue Greenfield and David Hargreaves

Los Angeles | London | New Delhi
Singapore | Washington DC

SAGE Publications Ltd
1 Oliver's Yard
55 City Road
London EC1Y 1SP

SAGE Publications Inc.
2455 Teller Road
Thousand Oaks, California 91320

SAGE Publications India Pvt Ltd
B 1/I 1 Mohan Cooperative Industrial Area
Mathura Road
New Delhi 110 044

SAGE Publications Asia-Pacific Pte Ltd
3 Church Street
#10-04 Samsung Hub
Singapore 049483

Library of Congress Control Number: 2011936154

British Library Cataloguing in Publication data
A catalogue record for this book is available from the British Library

ISBN 978-0-85702-731-3
ISBN 978-0-85702-732-0 (pbk)

Typeset by Dorwyn, Wells, Somerset
Printed in India by Replika Press Pvt Ltd
Printed on paper from sustainable resources

This book is dedicated to Kevin Brehony, who has been a constant source of help and support throughout the Froebel Research Fellowship project

Contents

Table

About the authors

Hiroko Fumoto is an Honorary Research Fellow of Roehampton University, and former Programme Convener for the MA in Early Childhood Studies. She trained originally as an early childhood teacher in Japan and has wide experience of working with young children in nursery schools in Japan and in the UK. For the last two years, she has been conducting research with early childhood teachers in the United States. Her research interests include teachers' perceptions of teacher–child relationships in early childhood settings (the topic of her doctoral studies), the influence of culture on early childhood practice, and professional development in the early childhood workforce. She has written journal articles and has presented a number of conference papers on related topics. She is also a member of the Editorial Board for *Early Years: International Journal of Research and Development*.

Sue Robson is Principal Lecturer and Head of Subject, Early Childhood Studies, at Roehampton University. She is a National Teaching Fellow and a Roehampton University Teaching Fellow. Sue has worked extensively in infant and nursery schools in London. Her particular research interests include the development of young children's thinking, ways of accessing young children's ideas and views, parent–professional relationships in early years settings, and the development of pedagogy in higher education. Sue has written books and journal articles on a wide range of aspects of early childhood, including *Education in Early Childhood: First Things First* (with Sue Smedley, 1996, Fulton), and 'The physical environment' in L. Miller, C. Cable and G. Goodliff (eds) *Supporting Children's Learning in the Early Years* (2nd edn, 2009, Routledge). In 2006 she published the highly successful book *Developing Thinking and Understanding in Young Children* (Routledge), now in its second edition.

Sue Greenfield is a Senior Lecturer in Early Childhood Studies at Roehampton. She trained as a nurse and worked in hospitals for several years before training as a Health Visitor working in London and in Surrey. She later gained experience of nursery settings, and was responsible for a 60-place nursery in Surrey for a number of years. She has been a member of the Froebel Research Fellowship team for three years and has given conference papers on this research in Reyjavik, Prague, Yokohama, and many different early childhood centres in the UK. Sue has written 'Working in multidisciplinary teams' in L. Miller and C. Cable (eds) *Professionalisation, Leadership and Management* (2010, Sage).

David J. Hargreaves is Professor of Education and Froebel Research Fellow in the Applied Music Research Centre at Roehampton University. He is a Chartered Psychologist and Fellow of the British Psychological Society. His books, which have been translated into 15 languages, include *The Developmental Psychology of Music* (1986, Cambridge University Press), *Children and the Arts* (1989, Open University Press), *Developmental Psychology and You* (with Julia Berryman, Martin Herbert and Ann Taylor, 1991, Routledge and BPS), *Musical Learning and Development: The International Perspective* (with Adrian North, 2001, Continuum), and *The Social and Applied Psychology of Music* (with Adrian North, 2008, Oxford University Press). He has also written numerous journal articles and book chapters in developmental and social psychology, music and education.

Acknowledgements

Over the years, numerous children, parents and early childhood practitioners have given generously of their time to share their experiences with us. They have invited us into their homes and to their early childhood settings, and openly let us share their lives with them. Without their generosity and commitment to promoting young children's creative thinking and well-being, this book would not have been possible. We are enormously grateful for all of their contributions and their interest in our work.

We are also indebted to our colleagues and students at Roehampton University. They helped develop our ideas by providing invaluable feedback during lectures and seminars. The discussions we have had over the years on creative thinking, parenting, early childhood pedagogy and research methodology, amongst other topics, have greatly challenged our thinking. We are indebted to the Froebel Research Committee, and to Dr Peter Weston in particular, for their financial and many other forms of support. We would especially like to thank Professors Kevin Brehony and Tina Bruce for their unfailing encouragement in the Early Childhood Research Centre at Roehampton University. Thanks are also due to Dr Victoria Rowe for help in collecting and analysing data, and for her supportive advice.

As for our friends and families – this work is the result of our joint efforts. Without them, we would not have been able to 'think creatively' enough to have completed this book. Our thanks go to all of them.

1

Introduction

Hiroko Fumoto and Sue Robson

This book explores theories, research and practice concerning young children's creative thinking, particularly in the context of their relationships with others. Whether we are parents, early childhood practitioners, teachers or researchers, we try to listen to children's thoughts and imagine what their understandings might be. We reflect on what we do with them, and wonder whether the environments that we create with them extend and stimulate their experiences. But what do we actually mean by creative thinking? Do we know when we see it in action? How do we go about investigating this? Importantly, what are the implications of understanding children's creative thinking for early childhood practice? We address these questions by placing children, parents and practitioners at the centre of our discussion in order to stress the significance of the collaborative environments that they create with one another.

Case study

John, a 5-year-old, arrives at school a little late with his father. He looks around the room where other children are all engaged in various activities, and says to himself with a grin: 'Everyone's playing a hundred games!' (cited in Fumoto, 2011: 27).

In the 3-year-olds' room, Thomas approaches his teacher, Ms Sheila, who is listening to Laura telling her a story, and says: 'I want to do some painting'. Sheila replies: 'Bring me a shirt and I'll help you put it on'. Thomas goes over to the easel and gets an old shirt that is used by the children when they paint and Sheila helps him

(Continues)

(Continued)

put it on. Thomas goes to the easel and turns around, and says: 'Ms Sheila, can you write my name?' Sheila responds: 'Why don't you get started because I'm talking to Laura now'. Thomas looks around and says 'OK' but does not start. He calls out again: 'Ms Sheila, can you write my name?' Sheila says with a smile: 'I'll come and write your name in a minute. Don't you worry'. Ms Sophie, an assistant teacher, walks over and writes his name instead. Thomas picks up a brush and starts to paint. Sheila laughs joyfully and says: 'Creative juice doesn't flow without his name!'

These are two children's experiences in an early childhood setting. John's comment makes us think about what children see, feel and think as they walk into their schools every morning. Thomas, who did not want to start painting until he had his name written on his paper, makes us wonder what might have been going through his mind as he looks at the white sheet of paper in front of him. Was John expressing his ownership of the environment, and Thomas, of his activity?

Our focus on social relationships in discussing children's creative thinking is by no means new. Indeed, historically, social relationships have been seen as the foundation of early childhood pedagogy. Friedrich Froebel (1782–1852), for instance, emphasized that the underpinnings of early childhood education were the 'unity' between and within individuals, and that children are more likely to follow their 'self-active instincts' when the relationships they form in early childhood settings resemble those of a loving family environment (Froebel, 1888). Liebschner (1992) suggests that, for Froebel, education is equivalent to the process of children and teachers living in harmony based on their mutual respect. The aim of Robert Owen (1771–1858), who established the UK's first nursery-infant school at New Lanark in 1816, was also 'to create communities made up of people who are motivated by the principle of mutual consideration, and who could live together in harmony' (Bradburn, 1967: 22). The idea of respect between children and teachers has also been the basis of work carried out by pioneers of early education such as Maria Montessori (1870–1952), and Rachel and Margaret McMillan (1859–1917, 1860–1931, respectively) (e.g. McMillan, 1930). More recently, Malaguzzi's (1993) *Reggio Emilia* approach, promoting children's intellectual development through its focus on symbolic representations of the world, has also emphasized that 'the three protagonists – children, teachers, and parents' are seen as the underpinnings of learning in early childhood settings (Edwards et al., 1998: 9).

This book builds on this historical basis of early childhood practice and demonstrates not only the uniqueness of children's, parents' and practitioners' experiences, but also the methodological and theoretical complexities involved in understanding them. To this end, we draw on materials collected through the Froebel Research Fellowship project, *The Voice of the Child: Ownership and Autonomy in Early Learning (FRF): 2002–present*, (see Froebel Educational Institute: http://www.froebel. org.uk/ fre.html) funded by the Froebel Educational Institute, and conducted by the authors. The project derives from our distinct but overlapping research interests: young children's thinking (Sue Robson), parent partnership in early childhood settings (Sue Greenfield), teacher–child relationships (Hiroko Fumoto) and creativity (David J. Hargreaves). Through collaboration, we have brought together our areas of interest in order to further our understanding of the ways in which we can promote the development of young children's creative thinking, and develop new ways of looking at young children's activity.

In the FRF project, we have had the pleasure of listening to children who have enthused us with the ways in which they express their creative thinking. Practitioners and parents have also inspired us with their dedication to supporting children's learning and development. They have shared with us the joy of observing, and being part of, children's thinking, as well as their anxieties. For instance, practitioners have told us of their frustration with the structural and curricular constraints that they encounter which put strain on providing what they believe is the 'best' environment for promoting children's thinking (Robson and Fumoto, 2009). Many parents have also voiced their concerns about not knowing enough of what children are doing at school. In this context, practitioners and parents have repeatedly raised the importance of the nature of social relationships in early childhood settings. Their views have motivated us to look further into the link between children's creative thinking and social relationships, and to think carefully about how we, as researchers, collaborate with them.

The early childhood field and creativity research

In recent years, the fields of early childhood and creativity research have undergone considerable development and change in terms of the ways in which we understand young children's development and learning, and how we conceptualize creativity. These changes have proved to be particularly relevant to the ways in which we explore children's creative thinking in early childhood settings. For instance, creativity, once seen as an ability that is possessed only by 'exceptional' individuals, is now seen as inherently present in all of us, including young children. Creative thinking is increasingly seen as permeating our everyday life through the ways in which we confront difficulties, think of new possibilities, and engage with our physical and social environments. It touches the realms of empathy, wisdom and social responsibility. The necessity for thinking and expressing our creativity is now considered as crucial for our own as well as for our collective well-being in society (e.g. Craft et al., 2008c). In particular, Craft's notion of 'possibility thinking' as an aspect of creativity, which encourages children to think of 'what if' questions, has been important for early childhood practice as it adopts a 'learner-inclusive approach' through emphasizing the importance of collaborative enquiry (e.g. Craft, 2002).

As creativity research has come to talk about 'democratic', 'wise' and 'good' creativity, demonstrating the shift from an individualized approach to a process that is embedded within the social aspects of our society (Craft et al., 2008c), so the early childhood field now also embraces the complexities of children's lives and their development, both in practice as well as in research. As Fleer and Robbins (2007) argue, the field has moved on from the developmental-constructivist tradition to incorporating cultural-historical or socio-cultural perspectives on children's development. Children's lives are no longer approached simply from the 'developmental milestone' view which takes them out of their contexts, but are understood as being embedded in their families, society, culture and history, highlighting the diversity of their experiences. Early childhood provisions are increasingly seen as settings in which children's learning is facilitated through 'communities of learners' which promote the process of creating the environment *with* children rather than from an adult-led agenda (Rogoff et al., 2001). In line with this, there are strong advocates for ethnographic approaches to research that consider these provisions as 'a cultural reality embedded deeply in the social fabric of everyday life – for both children *and* their caregivers' (Buchbinder et al., 2006: 46). These ways of understanding a child reflect an ecological model of human development (Bronfenbrenner, 1979) and the approach of life-span developmental psychology (Lerner, 2002), which remind us that a child's existence is intimately related to his/her physical and social environment: these approaches also resonate with socio-cultural theory (e.g. Rogoff, 2003; Vygotsky, 1978) and developmental systems theory (Ford and Lerner, 1992; Lerner, 2002), upon which this book draws. The implication of these changes is that young children's creative thinking cannot be understood without considering the ways in which it is shaped by their social relationships, and vice versa.

Policy and curriculum: international perspectives

Internationally, at policy and curricular level, there is clear evidence of the valuing of creativity, and of supporting young children's creative thinking, for both its present and future importance in their development. The Organisation for Economic Cooperation and Development (OECD) review of 2004, for example, which features a number of well-known early childhood education and care curriculum outlines from around the world, cites 'creativity' as something that should always be present in an Early Childhood Education and Care (ECEC) programme, ranking it alongside other aspects such as children's questions, exploration, fantasy and challenge (OECD, 2004). In the same publication, Laevers identifies the development of (future) adults who, amongst other things, are creative, as one of the key aims of the Belgian Experiential Education (EXE) programme. Vecchi links creativity and the place of the atelier, or studio, with pedagogical identity in Reggio Emilia, invoking Malaguzzi's view that the atelier should 'act as guarantor for the freshness and originality of an approach to things' (Vecchi, 2010: 1).

There is also strong evidence in curriculum documentation of the linkage between creativity and creative thinking and young children's opportunities to communicate and represent their experiences with others. In the Republic of Ireland, *Aistear*, the Early Childhood Curriculum Framework (NCCA, 2009), cites the importance of creative thinking and creativity in all four of its themes of well-being, communicating, identity and belonging, and exploring and thinking. However, the strongest links are made in the theme of communicating, with Aim 4 being that 'Children will express themselves creatively and imaginatively' (NCCA, 2009: 35). This includes through language, visual arts, music, problem solving, pretence and role play. This breadth is similar to both the Reggio Emilia idea of the 'hundred languages of children' (Edwards et al., 1998) and the Communication strand of the New Zealand *Te Whāriki* Early Childhood Curriculum which specifies, as one of four goals, the provision of an environment in which children can 'discover and develop different ways to be creative and expressive' (Ministry of Education, New Zealand, 1996: 80). These ways encompass all forms of expression, including pretend and dramatic play.

Policy and curriculum within the UK

Within the United Kingdom, government interest in ensuring that creativity is actively fostered in nurseries and schools across the whole age range has been evident in a number of initiatives. In England, the then Qualifications and Curriculum Authority published *Creativity: Find It, Promote It* (QCA, 2005). The English Office for Standards in Education, Children's Services and Skills (Ofsted) published a survey of creative approaches to learning in 44 schools (2010). Similarly, Her Majesty's Inspectors of Education in Scotland reported on evidence from inspections illustrating good practice in promoting creativity (HMIE, 2006). All three cases are efforts to ensure more widespread implementation of the practices described. The curriculum documents for young children of all four countries of the UK (England, Northern Ireland, Scotland and Wales) contain explicit reference to creativity, though much less to either creative thinking or even to creative learning. Strongest in this regard is the extensive 'Building the Curriculum' series from Scotland, as part of the *Curriculum for Excellence*. In this, the ability to 'think creatively and independently' (Learning and Teaching Scotland, 2008) is seen as part of being a successful learner. At the 'Early level', the development of creative thinking and learning are highlighted (Learning and Teaching Scotland, 2007, 2008), with creativity having parity with 'important themes such as enterprise, citizenship, sustainable development [and] international education' (Learning and Teaching Scotland, 2008: 23), to be developed in a range of contexts. Both the Welsh and English frameworks similarly suggest that creativity cuts across subjects: 'Children should be constantly developing their imagination and creativity across the curriculum' (Department for Children, Education, Lifelong Learning and Skills (Wales), 2008: 39), and that it is linked to many forms of representation: 'art, music, movement, dance, imaginative and role-play activities, mathematics and design and technology' (DCSF, 2008: 106). At the same time, however, both the Welsh and English frameworks identify an 'area of learning' called 'Creative Development', which locates creative activity within arts-based areas such as dance, music and drama. This leaves room for very different interpretations of what might constitute creative activity, and, albeit unwittingly, may continue to focus practitioners on these subjects as 'creative', to the possible detriment of others. This contrasts markedly with the Swedish Curriculum for the Pre-School, which describes creativity as one of a number of 'every-day-life-skill(s)' (Pramling in OECD, 2004: 23), to be seen as general, and a part of all subjects.

At the same time, this rediscovered emphasis on creativity raises some questions. For example, the title of the 2010 Ofsted report, *Learning: Creative Approaches that Raise Standards,* is significant in positioning creative thinking and learning as of value in so far as they do not conflict with a 'standards' agenda. In addition, whilst creativity may be valued as an approach, it is conspicuously absent in assessment requirements in the UK. The English *Practice Guidance for the Early Years Foundation Stage* (DCSF, 2008), for example, makes welcome mention throughout of the importance of extending young children's creativity, through play, and across the curriculum. However, the Early Years Foundation Stage Profile (QCA, 2008), designed to provide a summative assessment of children's achievement and competence at the end of the Foundation Stage, has no items which involve creativity or creative thinking, although the proposals in the Tickell Review (DfE, 2011) (see below) are more positive in this respect. Similarly, the Outcomes for the Welsh *Framework for Children's Learning for 3- to 7-year-olds in Wales* has just one reference to establishing how 'children use materials/resources and tools to make creative images' (Department for Children, Education, Lifelong Learning and Skills (Wales), 2008: 57). This may have the unfortunate impact of depressing the status of creative thinking, in the eyes of practitioners, parents and children alike. As Pramling suggests, 'When only small details are evaluated, a literacy/numeracy syllabus for instance, teachers tend to start training to teach these details, and the whole idea of fostering young children's thinking, reflection and creativity becomes lost!' (OECD, 2004: 29). Whilst we are not necessarily suggesting that assessing creativity will either improve children's knowledge, skill and understanding of it, nor enhance practitioners' efforts in developing it, Eisner's comment that 'our nets define what we shall catch' (1985: 6) is an important reminder that what is assessed is often what is valued. As Prentice (2000) suggests, one important rationale for focusing on creativity and creative thinking is to counter such a narrowing of curriculum emphasis.

In England, the Tickell Review of the Early Years Foundation Stage (DfE, 2011) was published in March 2011, and, at the time of writing, its proposals are being examined and discussed by practitioners, academics and policy makers. In the context of creative thinking, it is potentially encouraging. In particular, the review proposes replacing the current 'Creative development' area of learning with 'Expressive arts and design', as well as the creation of three 'characteristics of effective learning' (DfE, 2011): playing and exploring, active learning, and creating and thinking critically. These three 'enduring' characteristics are described as underpinning all areas of learning, 'play[ing] a central role in learning, and in being an effective learner' (DfE, 2011: 87). Crucially, they are also included in the proposed replacement EYFS Profile, thus helping to ensure that practitioners focus on them. The third characteristic, 'creating and thinking critically' has obvious links to creative thinking. However, what is most interesting to note is that the strands within all three characteristics reflect much of our approach in identifying and describing young children's creative thinking, as set out in this book. These strands include 'finding out and exploring', 'being involved and concentrating', 'keeping on trying', 'enjoying achieving what they set out to do', 'having their own ideas', 'using what they already know to learn new things' and 'choosing ways to do things and finding new ways' (DfE, 2011: 79). The *Analysing Children's Creative Thinking* (ACCT) Framework described in Chapter 8 includes similar items as aspects of creative thinking behaviour.

The aims of the book

The book has three aims. The first is to explore the meaning of creative thinking and its link with social relationships. Despite the political, curricular and social interest in the promotion of creative thinking in early childhood worldwide, there is still a lack of coherent understanding of the concept, especially where young children are concerned. This is problematic, as we found in the FRF project that the ways we interpret children's creative thinking seem to be directly relevant to the ways in which we talk about pedagogy, and about the enhancement of children's well-being (Robson and Hargreaves, 2005). In this book, we do not attempt to provide a straightforward definition of creative thinking. Rather, we critically review the current notion of creative thinking in an effort to bridge the gap in our understanding and raise questions about how we might go about promoting it.

The second aim is to critically evaluate the ways in which we engage children, parents and practitioners in research. In the FRF project, we have employed a wide range of approaches such as video-stimulated reflective dialogues, interviews, observations, questionnaires and a measurement instrument. By considering some of these approaches, we hope the book will help readers to reflect on the methods that they employ in their own work. We have paid particular attention to the ways we listen to the research participants. For instance, we have considered the ways in which we, as researchers, develop relationships with children, parents and practitioners, and the ethics of our entering into their everyday lives. We think that the issues examined in the book are also relevant to how practitioners, parents and children come to work together in early childhood settings.

The third aim is to contribute to the professional development of early childhood practitioners, both pre- and in-service, by raising pertinent questions that are useful for those who are in a position to influence early childhood practice directly. We do not attempt to provide a 'quick fix' solution to practice, but instead, explore theoretical and methodological complexities in understanding children's creative thinking and social relationships, without losing sight of what is important in day-to-day practice. In doing so, we are not arguing that the promotion of children's creative thinking and social relationships are the most important aspects of early childhood practice. Rather, we think that the promotion of children's creative thinking and social relationships are vital in enhancing the quality of early childhood practice as a whole, which matters to children's learning and development.

All of us, including academics, policy makers, parents and early childhood professionals, are trying to sustain and expand high quality early childhood provision. However, especially in times of economic uncertainty, the challenge of implementing this remains enormous. High quality provision does not come cheap, and there is a need for political commitment and investment if we are to provide quality experiences for all children. There are other difficulties that add to this challenge. For instance, Greenfield (2011) reports that communication between parents and practitioners is not always adequate in early childhood provision. Despite the increasing attention paid to the significance of parental involvement in early learning, in reality, this remains a complex challenge. In addition, through the FRF project, we have uncovered the frustration that practitioners in England experience about the lack of time available to engage in meaningful interactions with children (Fumoto and Robson, 2006). In the United States, there is also a growing unease in the early childhood profession about the diminishing opportunities available for children to play once they start Kindergarten as a result of the possible 'standard overload' experienced by the teachers (Miller and Almon, 2009; NAEYC, 2009). These difficulties are particularly worrying as meaningful interactions between children, parents and practitioners and the quality of play are key ingredients in promoting children's creative thinking. In this book, we argue especially for the importance of promoting ownership of and autonomy in learning in this process (Robson and Fumoto, 2009).

In summary, the book aims to contribute to the growing resources available to academics, undergraduate and postgraduate students and practitioners in Early Childhood Studies and other related fields. There are currently several 'how-to' textbooks that give us ideas about how children's creative thinking might be promoted. There is also an increasing volume of research-based literature that explores creative thinking in relation to social relationships based on its theoretical underpinnings. These two areas do not often converge, and so miss the opportunity of informing one another. This book attempts to bridge this gap by integrating theories, research and practice.

The case studies and data that illustrate our discussion are gathered mainly in early childhood settings in England, and in the United States where one of the authors is currently based. The settings involved in the studies were from the private, voluntary, independent and maintained sectors. Those who took part in the studies were children between 3 and 5 years of age, their parents and practitioners. The qualifications of practitioners in the studies included the English National Vocational Qualifications level 3, Qualified Teacher Status (degree level), Montessori Certificate and Masters in Early Childhood Studies, to name just a few. Their experience ranged from new entrants to the field to those who had been working with young children for over 20 years. What they had in common (apart from their interest in and support for the children!) was that all of them had responsibility for planning and implementing activities and young children's experiences in the setting.

Whilst the book is largely concerned with practice in the United Kingdom, the links that we are trying to make between conceptual aspects and practice are not limited to the UK. Indeed, the general concepts of creative thinking and social relationships cannot be considered without referring to other cultural interpretations. Accordingly, we explore these concepts from multiple perspectives, including those developed in Europe, Asia and elsewhere. This is particularly important as many early childhood settings involve children and families from culturally diverse communities, and because the practitioners themselves often come from different personal and professional backgrounds.

This book concerns young children, their parents, and the early childhood practitioners who work with them, by building on the literature that explores the development of thinking in children under 3 (e.g. Gopnik, 2009), amongst others. When we talk about parents, we include all primary caregivers. We also use terms such as 'teachers' and 'practitioners' interchangeably in order to make reference to a wide range of literature on those who work with young children and their families in their professional capacity.

How the book is organized

The book is in three main parts. In Part 1, we discuss the ways in which creativity and creative thinking can be conceptualized, and explore the links with young children's social relationships. While our focus is on the creative thinking that children express in their everyday lives, this does not mean that everything that children do is creative. We examine various ways of considering their creative thinking by taking a broadly social constructivist approach, highlighting its characteristics and diversity.

Part 2 addresses the methodological issues of investigating children's, parents' and practitioners' experiences. This includes the possible benefits of using approaches such as video-stimulated recall, which is becoming increasingly popular in eliciting young children's understanding of their own experiences. We also consider the complications of involving parents in research: of parents who are hard to reach, and those who speak English as an additional language. Another methodological issue that is highlighted in this section is the use of a mixed methods approach in early childhood research. In recent years, ethnographical and other methods have increasingly been seen as the key to understanding people's experiences, and 'democratic' ways of conducting research and co-constructing meanings with participants have been popularized along with the development of socio-cultural approaches to childhood. Part 2 explores how current research has developed the idea of conducting research *with* participants rather than *on* them, and considers the implications of this for mixed methods approaches.

Part 3 focuses on the experiences of children, parents and practitioners. It explores the ways in which these three protagonists engage with one another, and how they promote ownership and autonomy in their own and in others' learning and practice. First, young children's experience of their own creative thinking is explored by drawing on observations of children made in the FRF project, and by investigating the conversations that we, and the practitioners, had with children by means of video-stimulated dialogue with them. Detailed analyses of the video clips of children's day-to-day interactions with peers and adults, and also of their own surroundings, are presented in order to explore some of these new ways of understanding children's experiences.

Second, parents' understanding of young children's creative thinking is explored: this includes the opportunities that they provide at home for children to express their creativity and the difficulties they may experience when working along with practitioners to facilitate these opportunities. Third, the practitioners' perspectives on developing the environments that promote young children's expression of their creative thinking are examined. The ways in which some settings are able to overcome the structural constraints upon their interactions with children are presented so as to explore some realistic and productive ways of engaging meaningfully with children and their families.

The final chapter in Part 3 draws together the discussion, and considers its implications for early childhood practice and theoretical and methodological approaches towards understanding young children's creative thinking. We conclude with some thoughts for future research and thinking on the promotion of young children's creative thinking at home and at school.

Part 1

Creative Thinking, Social Relationships and Early Childhood Practice

The first part of this book consists of three chapters and provides the theoretical underpinning to what follows in Parts 2 and 3. In it we attempt to explain what is meant by creative thinking, and to explore some of the ways in which it is linked with social relationships in early childhood. In some ways, our attempts to clarify the meanings of creative thinking in young children may seem contradictory to the ways which we also advocate for looking for its diversity. What we aim to do in this opening section is to present 'young children's creative thinking' in all its complexity. As David J. Hargreaves writes at the outset (Chapter 2), creativity and creative thinking are indeed a 'huge topic' in the field of early childhood, and a potential minefield when it comes to defining them. Based on his years of experience in exploring creativity, he reviews a great deal of literature and research, and focuses on those parts of it that are particularly relevant to our current concern: that is, to promote young children's creative thinking. His chapter provides the groundwork to those which follow by describing the ways in which creativity has been studied over the years, and by evaluating its significance in early years and educational settings.

In Chapter 3, Sue Robson focuses our attention on creative thinking *in young children*. Certain characteristics are defining features of young children's creative thinking, and the chapter highlights some of the key issues that arise in identifying and analysing children's creative thinking. It also evaluates the importance of children's play, and the affective contexts that can support the development of their creativity, including provision of time, space and choice, amongst other issues.

In the final chapter of Part 1, Hiroko Fumoto and Sue Greenfield explore the relevance of social and cultural contexts in children's creative thinking. Whilst the significance of these contexts for children's development is touched upon throughout the book, this chapter focuses on explaining the ways in which social relationships and 'culture' are embedded in the development of children's creative thinking, which helps us to see the diverse nature of creative thinking itself. The chapter also examines the notion of communicative relationships between children, parents and teachers.

Each chapter includes a 'Reflection' that invites you, the reader to discuss your own thoughts about creative thinking, and we hope that all the chapters that follow will help you to reflect on your own local context and circumstances.

2

What do we mean by creativity and creative thinking?

David J. Hargreaves

> This chapter focuses on:
>
> - Some of the different definitions of creativity;
>
> - Distinguishing between studies of the person, the product, the process, and the environment in creativity research;
>
> - Evaluating the significance of creativity in early years and educational settings;
>
> - Reviewing some of the psychological approaches to creativity.

There is general agreement in many different fields of endeavour, and in many different parts of the world, that creativity is very important. The human capacity to adapt to new situations, and to produce new innovations in ever-changing conditions, is fundamental to our existence. For example, creativity is currently seen in some Asian countries as essential for industrial production and economic growth: being able to come up with new ideas in manufacturing or different ways of working are central to developments in business and management. In this particular field, ideas like lateral thinking (de Bono, 1968) and brainstorming (Osborn, 1953) were devised as ways of stimulating creativity, and have entered the public arena.

Creativity is often associated with the arts in many people's minds: we think of acknowledged artistic geniuses like Mozart, Dylan Thomas, or Van

Gogh as showing extremely high levels of creativity. All of these three famous creators were well known for their troubled personal lives, and this helps to fuel the popular image of tortured creative artists whose insecurity and unhappiness are expressed in and resolved through their art. In fact, this myth can be debunked in two ways: first, scientists, historians, or politicians can be just as creative as artists; and a look at the list of recent Nobel prizewinners would quickly show that they don't necessarily have troubled personal lives. Second, creativity does not have to exist at high levels of achievement in a particular chosen field: we all can and do display creativity at lower levels in our everyday lives. The term 'everyday creativity' has been used to describe this (see Richards, 2010).

In this chapter we first address the difficult and long-standing questions of defining and investigating creativity, and then look at two main areas which are particularly important for our work on the FRF project. The first is the huge topic of creativity in the early years as well as throughout childhood, which is important from both the theoretical and the practical points of view, and which forms the backdrop to this book. The second area is the study and explanation of creativity within psychology. Psychological studies of creativity have been undertaken for many years: many theoretical approaches have been developed, and empirical studies carried out. This area has also been given a boost in recent years by the rapid growth of cognitive neuroscience, in which research is beginning to suggest that there may be a neural basis for creativity (see e.g. Brattico and Tervaniemi, 2010).

Defining creativity

There is an inherent difficulty in trying to define creativity, because its essence is to go beyond the bounds of what is already given. Plato (Merleau-Ponty, 1962: 371) put it like this:

> How will you set about looking for that thing, the nature of which is totally unknown to you? Which among the things you do not know is the one you propose to look for? And if by chance you should stumble upon it, how will you know that it is indeed that thing, since you are in ignorance of it?

It seems to follow from this that our definitions need to be context-specific: that they need to refer to the production of solutions to specific problems, in specific situations, within specific social and cultural contexts. When creativity is not 'grounded' in this way, the term becomes over-used and abused: Liam Hudson (1966: 119) suggested that 'In some circles "creative" does duty as a word of general approbation – meaning, approximately, "good" ... [it] covers everything from the answers to a particular kind of psychological test, to forming a good relationship with one's wife'.

Before looking at these issues in more depth, it may be helpful to look at some of the definitions of creativity which have been put forward by some leading contemporary theoreticians and educators. Most of these include the use of original thinking, along with the application of that original thinking to specific practical solutions. Four definitions by prominent figures are shown below:

- Margaret Boden (1999: 351): 'Creativity is the generation of ideas that are both novel and valuable';

- Philip Johnson-Laird (1988: 203): 'mental processes that lead to solutions, ideas, conceptualisations, artistic forms, theories or products that are unique and novel';

- Ken Robinson (NACCCE, 1999: 30): 'Imaginative activity fashioned so as to produce outcomes that are both original and of value';

- James Kaufman and Robert Sternberg (2007: 55): 'A creative response to a problem is new, good, and relevant'.

Although these definitions have a lot in common, they nevertheless focus on different aspects of creativity. Johnson-Laird and Robinson's definitions are based on the *process* of creativity; Boden's definition is based on the *person* who is being creative; and Kaufman and Sternberg's definition is concerned with the *products* of creativity. Alongside these three aspects, we also need to consider the *place* (environment) in which creativity takes place: these are the four main dimensions of creativity research. To these traditional 'four Ps' of creativity, Simonton (1990) added *persuasion*, which is based on the idea that in order to be recognized as creative, individuals have to influence how other people think, that is, to be persuasive; and Runco (2007) added *potential*, which refers to the distinction between the capacity to become creative given appropriate conditions, and the manifest performance of creativity.

The title of this book is 'Young children's creative thinking', and that of this chapter makes a distinction between creative thinking and creativity itself: this deserves some comment at the outset. It is already clear that creativity can be defined so broadly that it effectively refers to 'an indefinite number of related concepts or behaviours' (Cook, in press) – it may make more sense to talk about a range of 'creativities'. In the FRF we focus on aspects of young children's behaviour, and make the implicit inference that certain types of behaviour indicate creative thinking in young children: following Robert Sternberg's approach, we suggest that the most important of these are: (a) the motivation to take on new challenges; (b) the motivation to engage in activities they enjoy doing; and (c) the motivation to persist. We have followed this approach by establishing our own observational framework, the ACCT (*Analysing Children's Creative Thinking*) Framework, which is intended to identify the behavioural antecedents of creative thinking. The next inferential leap is to suggest that creative thinking is a predictor of real-life creativity when linked with optimal environmental conditions, and appropriate levels of motivation and persistence. Young children's behaviour may display 'mini-c' creativity, which is described in the next section below, in which we will look at the four traditional dimensions in turn – the *person*, the *product*, the *process*, and the *environment*.

The person, the product, the process, and the environment in creativity research

Studies of creativity which focus on the *person* have largely concerned people's cognitive styles, and their personality characteristics. The distinction which predominated in the upsurge of studies on 'creativity testing' in the 1960s and 1970s was that between convergent and divergent thinking: the former involves the ability to come up with the one correct answer to a problem such as 'what is the next number in the sequence 2, 4, 7, 11 ...', which involves logical, deductive thinking. Divergent thinking, on the other hand, is concerned with the generation of many different solutions to an open-ended problem, such as 'how many uses can you think of for a melon?' In the early literature (e.g. Getzels and Jackson, 1962; Wallach and Kogan, 1965), creativity was associated with divergent thinking, and convergent thinking with intelligence, but that was soon seen to be mistaken, as real-life creativity involves both convergent *and* divergent abilities.

Several different personality factors have also been proposed as being characteristic of creative thinkers, in particular independence, non-conformity and confidence, and studies have been carried out to relate people's scores on these tests to those on 'creativity tests'. Research using this psychometric approach eventually began to decline in popularity with the increasing realization that creativity is not a stable characteristic of individuals which can be measured in a test; in fact, it can only really be identified in relation to specific situations and contexts.

Our second main area of research is that which focuses on creative *products* within specific situations: in studying children's creativity in the classroom, for example, one might focus on different individual responses to actual tasks such as those in writing, drawing, or music. Teresa Amabile (Amabile, 1996) recommends this kind of approach in what she calls a 'consensual assessment technique': products are judged as creative or not on the basis of the extent to which experts in that area regard them as such. We will return to Amabile's approach in the fourth section of this chapter, on psychological approaches to creativity.

The third approach is to look at the *process* of creativity: one well-known and widely quoted model is that first proposed by Graham Wallas (1926), who suggested that there are four main stages of the creative process, namely: *preparation* for the problem area by immersing oneself in the problem area; *incubation*, the mysterious process in which no conscious work is done, but in which different connections and reflections develop unconsciously; *illumination*, the 'eureka' moment at which the realization of the creative solution suddenly dawns on the creator; and *verification*, in which the creative solution is worked out in the practical terms of the problem area. This four-stage model is a simplified version of Wallas's original seven-stage model, which included *encounter*, *concentration* and *persuasion* as the first, third and final stages respectively, while Koberg and Bagnall (1991) proposed a more recent seven-stage model, which involved *accepting the challenge, analysing, defining, ideating, selecting, implementing* and *evaluating*.

Finally, studies have been undertaken of the particular contexts and *environments* in which creativity takes place, and there are two quite distinct ways of looking at this, which rely on the distinction between what has been called 'small c' and 'big C' creativity (see e.g. Gardner, 1993). The former refers to what we described earlier on as 'everyday creativity', which we experience in our daily lives, whereas the latter refers to the kinds of breakthrough which only occur in great thinkers such as Einstein, Debussy or Picasso. Boden (1999) makes a similar distinction between what she calls P(sychological) creativity – for example, the formulation of an idea that might be new to a particular person, but which many others may have had before, and H(istorical) creativity, which applies to ideas which are novel with respect to the whole of human history. Historical (or big C) creativity is concerned with the effects of social and cultural factors on the development and emergence of unique ideas in a particular and influential creative thinker. Kaufman and Beghetto (2009) recently suggested adding two further types: 'mini-c' creativity, which is a precursor of small c or even big C creativity that can be seen in the very young, and 'pro-c' creativity, which is somewhere in between small c and big C in that those displaying it have developed sufficient levels of skill and motivation to make genuine creative contributions to their field, but do not do so at the level of big C.

Explaining the ways in which cultural, social and situational contexts affect individual thinking is the main focus of the socio-cultural approach in developmental social psychology, which originated in the work of Lev Vygotsky (e.g. Vygotsky, 1966). Socio-cultural theory enables the explanation of interpersonal and broader environmental influences on many aspects of behaviour: two prominent examples are how language is used to mediate what Mercer (2000) calls 'interthinking' in social groups, and the ways in which this can explain how members of small groups interact with one another in collaborative creativity (see e.g. Miell and Littleton, 2004; Sawyer, 2003, 2010). It follows that there is a great deal of cultural diversity in the many possible manifestations of creativity, although Lubart (2010) points out that Western paradigms tend to have predominated in the literature. He outlines various cross-cultural perspectives on creativity, and Kaufman and Sternberg's (2006) *International Handbook of Creativity* is devoted to the same end.

To summarize this section, we can see that there are many different ways of defining, conceptualizing and explaining creativity. It is possible to investigate the products of real-life creativity, as we have seen above: but the main emphasis has been on the *processes* involved. Our own emphasis in this book is on creative thinking in young children, and on its behavioural manifestations in particular. Creative thinking is much more difficult to identify in young children than at other ages in the life span, partly because of their relative immaturity with respect to language, and also because creative activities in later life are far more circumscribed and domain-specific. It follows that one important aim of early years education should be to provide young children with the autonomy and motivation to express that creativity in their everyday activity: and this leads to the consideration of how this might best be accomplished.

Creativity in early years and other educational settings

From the practical/policy point of view, the promotion of creativity can be seen as something which comes into and goes out of fashion as social and political changes take place. In the UK, for example, nurturing children's creativity was seen as an important outcome of child-centred learning, and there were some notable (and some notorious) educational experiments in the 1960s and 1970s which achieved varying degrees of success. The tide turned when the Conservative governments of Margaret Thatcher and John Major came to power in the 1980s and 1990s, however, and the focus shifted to the idea of 'back to basics'. This was based on the view that children's command of the 'three Rs' (Reading, wRiting and aRithmetic) was badly in decline as a result of the 'progressive' ideas of the 1960s and 1970s, and that it was more important to produce children who could read, write and do arithmetic than to be concerned about abstract aims such as fostering creativity and independence of thought.

In the new century, however, the pendulum of fashion has swung back once again: creativity is high on the agenda in education, and in educational research. In the UK, the National Advisory Committee on Creative and Cultural Education (NACCCE) was established in 1998 by the Secretary of State for Education and Employment to review 'the creative and cultural development of young people through formal and informal education', and this led to *All Our Futures: Creativity, Culture and Education* (NACCCE, 1999: 2), a government report which strongly emphasized the importance of the creative and cultural development of young people through formal and informal education. This report made numerous detailed recommendations about the ways in which creative and cultural education can be used to promote the personal, intellectual, social and economic development of young people, and thereby improve their future leisure and work opportunities; it has had a long-lasting impact on educational policy and practice since it was first published.

As we saw in Chapter 1, there is a good deal of emphasis on the promotion of creativity in the curricula which have been suggested for young children in all four countries of the UK (England, Northern Ireland, Scotland and Wales). In England, 'Creative development' is one of the six main areas in the Statutory Framework for the Early Years Foundation Stage (DCSF, 2008): but in spite of the recognition that creativity should cut right across the curriculum, and be fostered in non-arts subjects like maths or science, for example, there nevertheless remains a strong tendency to associate creativity with the arts.

This level of interest in and emphasis on the practical importance of creativity is also reflected in the academic literature on education. Various educational research journals have published special issues on creativity in the last decade, including, for example, the *Cambridge Journal of Education* (2006) and the *International Journal of Educational Research* (2008), with a prevailing view in this literature being that creativity is present in all of us to varying degrees, and is not a characteristic that is only possessed by the gifted few. These ideas have been extended and developed: Craft (2002) was concerned with children's ability to formulate 'what if' questions in collaboration with others, for example, and Craft, Gardner and Claxton (2008c) suggested that the expression of creativity is central to our individual and collective well-being.

Baroness Susan Greenfield, a distinguished neuroscientist who contributed to the *All Our Futures* report in 1999, suggested (Greenfield, 2006) that research on the genetic and neurological processes underlying creativity should play a vital part in shaping these developments, and in doing so could throw light on the origins of other disorders including dyslexia: this remains an exciting prospect for the future. More recently, however, she has sounded a strong warning note (Greenfield, 2010a) by speculating about how children's avid adoption of the new technologies in computer games and the like could be depriving them of the benefits of real-life experiences:

> The human brain is exquisitely sensitive to the environment: a growing number of examples of this 'plasticity' suggest that the biological basis of the mind could be the personalisation of the brain through unique, dynamic configurations of

neuronal connections, driven in turn by unique experiences. Hence 'blowing' the mind could indeed describe the disabling of neuronal connectivity with psychotropic drugs ... This mind-set corresponds to the syndrome seen with a hypo-functional prefrontal cortex where the individual has a short attention span, is less risk averse, living for the moment, and viewing the world literally ... it is possible that excessive exposure to screen experiences, characterised by frequent audio-visual overload and high arousal could drive the young brain into a configuration characterised by an underactive prefrontal cortex ... persistent use of new technologies could be in themselves preferred to 3-dimensional, real experiences and in turn have the potential to retain the brain in an immature mind-set.

Although the new technologies clearly have massive potential for promoting children's creativity in numerous ways, Greenfield's cautionary statement clearly indicates the importance of their use in ways which benefit all aspects of young children's development – the social and the emotional, as well as the cognitive. An important aspect of this is the network of social relationships which form the backdrop to children's creativity, and our focus in the FRF project on the effects of young children's social relationships on creative thinking will become apparent.

Psychological theories of and research on creativity

The early study of creativity in psychology was dominated by the cognitive tradition, its course having been set by J.P. Guilford's (1950) pioneering Presidential Address to the American Psychological Association: this is widely cited as having kick-started the growth of psychological research over the intervening half century. We might also add that the first ever publication of one of us (Hargreaves and Bolton, 1972), a factor analytic study using tests of divergent thinking, was inspired by this early surge of activity, which gives us almost a 40-year track record in this area!

Just as in the educational literature, a great deal of current interest and activity in creativity is also apparent in psychological research: this is illustrated by the American Psychological Association's launch of their new journal, *Psychology of Aesthetics, Creativity and the Arts* in 2006, as the house journal of Section 10 of the APA – the Society for the Psychology of Aesthetics, Creativity, and the Arts, which was founded in 1945. The most authoritative guide to the psychological literature on creativity for the last 10 years or so has been Sternberg's (1999) *Handbook of Creativity*: this was followed by Kaufman and Sternberg's (2006) *International Handbook of Creativity*, which focuses on international variations in this topic, and Kaufman and Sternberg (2010) have recently published *The Cambridge Handbook of Creativity*, which updates the field once more.

Sternberg and Lubart's opening chapter in the 1999 version of the handbook documents the main theoretical traditions within creativity research, which include biological, psychoanalytic, associative, psychometric, cognitive, computational, social-personality, and what they describe as confluence approaches, which include varying combinations of the former. Kozbelt, Beghetto and Runco's chapter on 'Theories of creativity' in the 2010 *Cambridge Handbook* extends this to a list of 10 theories, most of which are newly labelled, namely: developmental, psychometric, economic, stage and componential process, cognitive, problem-solving and expertise–based, problem-finding, evolutionary, typological and systems theories. We shall make no attempt to review or even to characterize all these theories here: instead, we focus on three specific approaches which are most relevant to the FRF project. We have been most interested in social-personality approaches, as well as in those in positive psychology, in which the child's well-being is accorded just as much importance as are cognitive advances. We devote the rest of this chapter to a brief consideration of three theories: Amabile's social-environmental theory, Csikszentmihalyi's flow theory, and Ryan and Deci's (2000) self-determination theory.

Teresa Amabile's book *The Social Psychology of Creativity* (1983) set out the main features of the social psychological approach, which she followed up and developed further in *Creativity in Context* (1996). At the broadest level, the social psychological approach focuses on the effects of contextual, environmental, social and cultural factors upon the development of learning and thought, which of course includes creativity. Amabile (1996) also emphasizes the importance of social-environmental factors in creativity, though her conception of these is rooted in a cognitive and experimental approach, and a strong interest in assessment and measurement, rather than in socio-cultural theory.

The last of these is closely related to the concept of intrinsic (as distinct from extrinsic) motivation, and this is one of the main tenets of Amabile's social psychological approach. Amabile (1996) adopts what she calls a 'componential framework' of creativity based on the three main components of domain-relevant skills, creativity-relevant skills, and task motivation, focusing in particular on the importance of *intrinsic motivation*. Her 'intrinsic motivation hypothesis' of creativity is that 'the intrinsically motivated state is conducive to creativity, whereas the extrinsically motivated state is detrimental' (1996: 107). Her own research, and that of her associates, includes experimental and psychometric studies which generally confirm this idea. Amabile's version of the social psychological approach nevertheless has little to say about the emotional and affective aspects of creativity, which in our view form a vital part of it.

One general approach which specifically focuses on the emotional and affective aspects of behaviour is that of positive psychology: this is a relatively new field of study, which was launched in 1998 when Martin

Seligman chose it as the theme for his Presidential Address to the American Psychological Association (see Seligman and Csikszentmihalyi, 2000). One of the main ideas in this field is the importance of promoting people's sense of well-being, and subjective well-being is seen as having two main aspects. The distinction between these was first enunciated by Aristotle: the first is the 'hedonic' aspect, which involves happiness, positive moods and emotions. However, simply being happy is not in itself sufficient to induce subjective well-being, as people also need the second, 'eudaimonic' aspect: this involves feelings of self-worth, purpose and fulfilment. Thus, life satisfaction is gained through achieving happiness, as well as engaging successfully in those activities which one personally values highly.

It is easy to see how creativity could fulfil people's eudaimonic needs, and also possibly some of their hedonic ones. Creativity is frequently seen as being strongly associated with self-esteem and well-being: a creative individual engages in creative activities for their own sake, and for the feelings of self-development and worthiness that they engender, and this is essentially the same as Amabile's intrinsic motivation. A recent study of creative musicians (composers and improvisers) by Chapman (2006), for example, showed that financial rewards were hardly ever mentioned as a motivation for the work they do; their satisfaction and sense of purpose arises as an intrinsic part of the activities themselves.

This idea is also captured by Mihaly Csikszentmihalyi's (1996) idea of *flow* in creative activities: flow is a state which occurs when we are so involved in and concentrated upon what we are doing that awareness of the rest of the world seems to disappear – long periods of time may pass without us noticing. This is reported in many activities, by writers, by improvising jazz musicians, by mountain climbers and athletes (who speak of being 'in the zone'), for example. The explanation of creativity is a central part of Csikszentmihalyi's approach.

The idea of flow has also been applied to young children's play activities: whether playing with others, or individually, they can become so engrossed in particular episodes of fantasy or make-believe activity that their behaviour clearly exhibits flow as described above: and this has been shown to be associated with creative thinking. In the field of young children's music learning, Custodero (in press) suggests that 'the compelling nature of musical materials – melodic contours, rhythmic vitality, phrase structures, and harmonic intensity – invites participation, and thereby offers opportunities for *creative action*'. Custodero (2005) devised several observable indicators of flow in young children's music learning that gave them a sense of creative empowerment, and she has discussed how observational studies of flow experience in music education settings can give direct insight into their creative thinking in music.

Another 'social-personality' theory approach which is also in tune with the aims of positive psychology is Ryan and Deci's (2000) *self-determination theory*. This holds that when the basic psychological needs of *relatedness*, *competence* and *autonomy* are satisfied, motivation and well-being are enhanced. Relatedness refers to a person's activities taking place within a social network, and thereby being influenced by the social and cultural context: this takes us back to socio-cultural theory, mentioned above. Competence refers to the cognitive aspects of engagement in creative activities – one needs to have mastered the basic skills and concepts of that domain of activity. Autonomy, which in a sense is encapsulated in the term 'self-determination', means that our creative activities are likely to be most highly motivated when they are generated by ourselves, rather than by external demands or by other people. Once again, we can see that young children's creative play can readily fulfil all three of these basic needs, and when this is the case, their self-determination, intrinsic motivation and subjective well-being are enhanced.

Conclusion

In this chapter we have raised some of the many problems and conceptual issues involved in the long-standing and thorny problem of trying to define creativity. We have considered why the development of children's creativity is so important in early years and other educational settings, and have looked at some of the educational research on the topic – our own FRF research will be covered in more detail later in the book. We have also looked at the extensive psychological literature on creativity, focusing in particular on those theories which can help us to explain young children's creative thinking, especially as manifested in their behaviour.

In conclusion, we suggest that young children's creative thinking needs four distinct foundations: each one of these needs to be present in children's lives for creativity to flourish. First, *social* foundations are needed: young children's friendships and peer relationships, as well as their social relationships with adults, are vital for the development of creative thinking. Secondly, creativity requires *cognitive* foundations: creative play provides an arena in which the abilities, skills and competencies required for creative thinking are fostered and developed. Thirdly, *emotional* foundations are necessary: children's well-being is an essential precursor of creative thinking, and the field of positive psychology can provide important insights into how this actually works in practice. Fourthly and finally, creative thinking needs *motivational* foundations, and intrinsic motivation in particular: children engage in creative activities for their own sake rather than for any extrinsic reward or benefit, and these enhance their feelings of self-esteem and well-being.

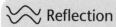 Reflection

Identify a person* that you consider to be creative, or especially talented in some way: this could be someone you know personally, or a famous figure from the past or present. Think about her development and current status: what factors shaped her development? Try to answer this in terms of the '6 Ps' of creativity:

- *Potential*: were there any signs of their later development in her childhood?
- *Person*: what distinctive aspects of her personality contribute to her creativity?
- *Process*: what is distinctive about the way in which she works?
- *Product*: what is distinctive about her creative output?
- *Place*: what aspects of her environment have contributed to her creativity?
- *Persuasion*: what effects does her creative work have on those around her?

*For clarity of expression I have used an individual for this example, who needs a gender: as the only male author of the book my arbitrary choice had to be a female!

3

Creative thinking in early childhood

Sue Robson

This chapter focuses on:

- What we mean by creative thinking in young children and its links to critical thinking and problem solving;

- Approaches to developing children's thinking;

- Characteristics of young children's creative thinking;

- Affective contexts for supporting and extending young children's creative thinking;

- Space, time and choice in young children's creative thinking;

- Play and pretence;

- Communication and language and young children's creative thinking.

What do we mean by creative thinking in young children?

David J. Hargreaves's examination of creativity and creative thinking in Chapter 2 forms a backdrop for the discussion here, which looks in more detail at creative thinking in young children. In particular, this chapter looks at how creative thinking relates to other types of thinking and the more recently emergent notion of 'creative learning' (Craft et al., 2008a).

27

It considers how the social, cognitive, emotional and motivational foundations of young children's thinking can be built upon in practice.

As we have argued in Chapter 2, creative thinking is part of everyday life for young children, and is neither the preserve of 'creative' people nor exclusively located in 'the arts'. We argue, along with Siraj-Blatchford (2007: 7) that 'creativity is a universal capability', and that everyone has creative potential (Runco, 2003). When looked at in this way, creativity, and creative thinking, become everyday events (Richards, 2006) in the lives of young children, and are often referred to as 'little c creativity' (Craft, 2003; Kaufmann, 2003).

Our starting point is that all acts of creativity must involve some creative thinking. The NACCCE definition of creativity cited in Chapter 2 as 'imaginative activity fashioned so as to produce outcomes that are both original and of value' (1999: 29) encapsulates many of the commonly accepted characteristics of creativity. Sternberg defines *creative thinking* as 'thinking that is novel and that produces ideas that are of value' (2003: 325–6). Sternberg's use of 'novelty' rather than 'originality' is significant in clarifying that, to count as creative, someone's idea does not have to embody thinking that has never been done before by anyone. Rather, creative thinking is thinking which is new for *that individual*, not necessarily for society as a whole, a point of particular significance when looking at young children's creative thinking. Kaufmann (2003) asserts that this 'subjective novelty', and the processes it embodies, is just as important as those of an objective novelty. Looked at in this way, whilst identifying whether any particular idea or act of a child is new for them will always be a challenge, it at least affords the possibility of recognizing young children's potential and their originality.

Whilst the NACCCE implicitly focuses on something tangible, Sternberg identifies ideas as the outcome of creative thinking. This has some similarities with Craft et al.'s definition of *creative learning* as 'significant imaginative achievement as evidenced in the creation of new knowledge' (Craft et al., 2006, cited in Craft et al., 2008a: xxi).

The other key idea common to both Sternberg's (2003) and the NACCCE's (1999) definitions is the notion of value. This has two implications. First, it views creative thinking as inherently social, and second, it highlights the connections between creative thinking and both so-called 'critical thinking', and problem solving. Looking at the first implication, the identification of something as 'creative' involves a value judgement. Amabile (1996: 33) suggests that 'A product or response is creative to the extent that appropriate observers independently agree it is creative'. She sees domain familiarity as the qualification for being an 'appropriate observer'. In the context of educational settings for young children, this could potentially include both adults and other children.

Creative thinking, critical thinking and problem solving

The second implication of the idea of value links creative thinking with critical thinking and problem solving. Whilst Sternberg (2003: 335) suggests that creative thinking is 'relatively distinct from analytical or practical thinking' as sets of skills, nevertheless, choices and critical evaluations are made by both participants and observers as part of any creative process. The NACCCE (1999: 31) talks of 'generative and evaluative thinking', and suggests that 'creative thinking always involves some critical thinking', whilst Lipman (2003) believes them to be interdependent. For Wright (2010), creativity is about both problem setting and problem solving, with meaningful solutions being formed about issues of relevance to the children involved.

Characteristics of creative thinking

In Chapter 2 we identified the work of Robert Sternberg as particularly helpful in thinking about creative thinking. Sternberg (2003: 333–5) identifies some key 'decisions' that, in his view, underlie creative thinking:

1. Redefine problems.
2. Analyse your own ideas.
3. Sell your ideas.
4. Knowledge is a double-edged sword.
5. Surmount obstacles.
6. Take sensible risks.
7. Willingness to grow.
8. Believe in yourself.
9. Tolerance of ambiguity.
10. Find what you love to do and do it.
11. Allowing time.
12. Allowing mistakes.

In the FRF project, we used Sternberg's 'decisions', along with a range of the other perspectives discussed here, as the starting point for developing the Analysing Children's Creative Thinking (ACCT) framework for identifying creative thinking in the behaviour of young children. This framework, looked at in more detail in Chapter 8, contains three categories: Exploration, Involvement and Enjoyment, and Persistence, each comprising a set of characteristics (see Table 8.1). These characteristics include aspects of divergent thinking, particularly flexibility and originality, which, along with imagination, are often cited as key attributes of creativity. However, the model of creative thinking which underpins the framework is not limited to ideas of divergence, and takes a broader perspective which recognizes that creative thinking can also be the product of convergent thinking (Dietrich, 2007), as discussed in Chapter 2, and that divergent thinking does not, of itself, necessarily lead to creative thought.

The aspects of young children's behaviour set out in the framework shown in Table 8.1 are helpful indicators in identifying creative thinking, albeit not unique to it. For example, Sternberg's 'analyse your own ideas' clearly has much in common with processes identified as indicating self-regulation (Bronson, 2000). They also highlight that identification of creative thinking behaviour, and opportunities for adults to support its development, will arise from young children's familiar activities and contexts.

Approaches to developing young children's thinking

In recent years there has been growing interest in the explicit development of young children's thinking. Two significant Department for Education and Skills Research Reports in England, for example (Moyles et al., 2002; Siraj-Blatchford et al., 2002), both investigated ways to develop young children's thinking as part of their brief. McGuinness (1999) categorizes the wide range of programmes designed for children of varying ages into three models for delivering thinking skills:

- Interventions directed towards enhancing thinking skills through structured programmes which are additional to the normal curriculum;

- Approaches that target subject-specific learning such as science and mathematics;

- Infusion across the curriculum through systematic identification of opportunities for thinking skills development within the normal curriculum.

(Adapted from McGuinness, 1999)

Trickey and Topping (2004) also identify a fourth category of 'Multi-method' programmes, which includes approaches such as Dawes, Mercer and Wegerif's *Thinking Together* (2000), and 'Philosophy for Children' (Lipman et al., 1980; Lipman, 2003).

Are some models more effective than others – particularly with young children?

Looking at the first model in McGuinness's categorization, Claxton (2006) is critical of what he sees as a 'bolt on' approach, which, in his view, ghettoizes creative thinking. Coles and Robinson (1991) suggest that the main criticism of the model is that it is reductionist and fragmentary, with limited transfer of skills learnt to new contexts. The idea of transferability is central to it, and this has proved to be a major challenge with regard to children of all ages. McGuinness's second category of approaches which focus on discrete subject areas may also be less valuable, given the holistic nature of young children's learning. The third category in McGuinness's typology, which foregrounds young children's thinking across a 'normal' curriculum – for young children this would be their everyday experiences – is consistent with the model of creative thinking outlined earlier, and, as a result, may be most helpful when planning for its support and development.

In attempting to draw some lessons for practice, McGuinness (1999) suggests that the more successful approaches are directed at 'cognitive apprenticeship', which includes scaffolding techniques, and metacognitive and self-regulatory approaches (Thinking Skills Review Group, 2004; Whitebread, 2000a). Looking at young children specifically, the most successful interventions seem to be those which take an embedded approach (Whitebread, 2000a), which is consistent with very widely held views on the value of framing young children's learning in meaningful contexts (Donaldson, 1978). Vygotsky (2004) suggests that this emphasis on the known, and meaningful contexts, underpins young children's creative activity, as they use recalled experiences to imagine something new, and to innovate.

These approaches also emphasize talk and interaction (Thinking Skills Review Group, 2004), highlighting the value of adults modelling, questioning and making their own thinking explicit to the children, in contexts in which the children themselves are required to articulate their thinking, and can enjoy 'playing around with ideas' (Whitebread, 2000a: 155). The Thinking Skills Review Group (2004) suggests that more emphasis by adults on making pedagogical strategies such as reasoning more explicit when working with young children may be as beneficial as any particular programme. This focus on talk and interaction is also characteristic of many of the approaches identified in Trickey and Topping's 'multi-method' category (2004). Overall, the creation of an atmosphere in which talking *about* thinking happens, and in which children are encouraged to reflect on their thinking, may be most important.

Contexts for young children's creative thinking

To summarize, the messages from research and practice in young children's creative thinking, along with those on developing thinking, emphasize the importance of the following characteristics in the contexts for the development of young children's creative thinking:

- Opportunities for children to explore ideas and materials, and to make choices about activities;

- Opportunities for children to try out and play with ideas, to speculate and hypothesize, and to use their imaginations, both alone and with others;

- An atmosphere of risk taking, in which children are encouraged to persist and to complete their self-set challenges;

- The embedding of young children's learning in meaningful contexts – this will often be as part of their play;

- A 'cognitive apprenticeship' approach, which includes adults scaffolding, modelling, questioning, and making their own thinking explicit to the children;

- An emphasis on talk and interaction, including young children being encouraged to articulate their thinking and to reflect on their thinking and learning.

How can these ideas influence practice? Runco and Johnson (2002) assert that the development of creativity, and hence of creative thinking, in children is dependent partly upon the contexts (physical and affective) in which they participate. The remainder of this chapter looks at a variety of contexts which it is valuable to think about and plan for in supporting and developing young children's creative thinking. These contexts will be very different for individual children, and an important implication for practice would be to provide opportunities for the development of creative thinking in a wide range of contexts and 'subject' areas.

Case study: The broken broom

In this episode in a class of 4–5-year-olds in England, the children develop their own ideas and responses to a problem set for them by their teacher, Annalea. Look at the bullet points on contexts for developing young children's creative thinking above – how many are evident here?

Annalea has fixed a broomstick broken into two pieces to the ceiling in the classroom. When the children arrive, she sits down with them, saying she is not sure how it got there. She asks them for their ideas, and thoughts on what they can do about it. The children and Annalea discuss the children's ideas together:

'Maybe the witch got lost'

'Maybe she flew into our school and her broom broke'

'I've got an idea, we could make her another broom'

'We could make her a rocket instead'

'We can draw a map so that the witch can find her way to the broomstick'

'We could look for clues that the witch has left behind'.

The children go off. Some draw maps and make potions to help the witch find her broomstick, others go outside to look for 'clues', taking a digital camera with them to record their finds. Later that morning they download their pictures onto the computer to show the rest of the class, for further discussion and speculation. Tara and Alexa go to the creative area. Tara begins by trying to jump up and measure the length of the broom by spreading her hands wide underneath it. She rolls a sheet of paper into a tube, sticking it with tape. She does the same with another sheet of paper, then fixes both tubes together to create a 'stick' that looks about the same length as the original. She glues feathers into the end to emulate the straw 'bristles' on the broom. Her friend Alexa finds it hard to roll the paper, so Tara demonstrates, and together they make another broom.

The emotional context of supporting young children's creative thinking

The links between emotion and cognition are well established (Robson, 2006), and are as centrally important to the development of young children's creative thinking as they are to other aspects of cognition. Hobson (2002) argues that children learn to think creatively as a result of being part of a loving relationship from which, in infancy, they begin to see things from two perspectives: their own, and that of a primary caregiver. In so doing, a baby has to imagine this other perspective, an act which helps to open up a 'mental space' of possibilities which ultimately supports symbolic thinking. Craft et al. (2008b) extend this emphasis to the classroom, highlighting the importance of providing a loving, supportive and secure environment in which children's self-determination, involvement and risk taking is encouraged.

Sternberg suggests that, to a great extent, creative thinking is attitudinal:

'creative people are creative, in large part, because they have *decided* to be creative' (2003: 333, emphasis in original), suggesting a key role for moti-vation, particularly intrinsic motivation (Amabile, 1996), although extrinsic factors may sometimes assist creativity (Runco et al., 2011). Meadows (2006), similarly, identifies a number of potentially valuable atti-tudes. Amongst these are choosing challenges rather than avoiding them, tolerance of risk, and the ability to both confront uncertainty and enjoy complexity. Richards (2006) emphasizes the importance of being able to tolerate ambiguity. This implies a significant role for emotional qualities such as self-efficacy and self-esteem and mastery. Hypothesizing, and mak-ing leaps of the imagination, require confidence on the thinker's part, and a willingness to take risks.

This has clear implications for practice, requiring a supportive environ-ment in which taking risks in one's thinking is encouraged and valued, and in which building children's self-confidence is prioritized by teachers (Sarsani, 2008). When this is not the case, the effects of stress and pressure to perform may contribute to a narrowing of focus, and more interest in 'getting it right' than in taking risks and coming up with ideas and out-comes of originality and value (Claxton, 1999).

Social context and young children's creative thinking

The relationship between the social and cultural context and young chil-dren's creative thinking is considered in much more detail in Chapter 4, but it is useful to highlight some specific messages from research, theory and practice here.

The research and practice described throughout this book adopts a Vygotskian, socio-constructivist perspective, which foregrounds the ways in which young children's development, including the development of their thinking, cannot be separated from its social context. Central to the part played by social context in the development of young children's cre-ative thinking are the relationships created between participants. Sylva et al. (2010) emphasize the pivotal role played by adults, particularly highly qualified early childhood specialists, in supporting children's thinking through what they describe as 'sustained shared thinking': 'any episode in which two or more individuals 'worked together' to solve a problem, clar-ify a concept, evaluate activities, extend a narrative etc.' (Sylva et al., 2010: 157). Importantly, this process is inherently collaborative, an aspect high-lighted by others such as Claxton (2006) and Craft (2003). Siraj-Blatchford (2007) draws attention to research which suggests that young children's problem solving improves in collaboration, with the partners acting to scaffold one another's understanding. This also illustrates how collabora-tion may be between adults and children, but also between children themselves. Children in friendship pairs are more successful in problem-solving activities than non-friends (Smith et al., 2003). Even where they are not friends, children in novice–expert pairs can show significant improvements in their performance in problem-solving tasks (Katz and Chard, 2000). When adults are involved, children may sometimes be more likely to say that they cannot do something. When working with other children, they may often gain confidence through mimicking another child (Whitebread et al., 2005). What may be particularly significant is the quality of playful interaction between collaborators (Siraj-Blatchford, 2007).

At the same time, Lloyd and Howe's (2003) research with children of 4 and 5 years of age shows a positive association between solitary active play (solitary pretence and functional play with objects) and divergent thinking, an important element of creative thinking. They speculate that time to think things over, rehearse experiences, and possibly generate further possibilities, in solitude, may all be important in supporting divergent thinking skills. This seems to link with Claxton's ideas (building on Wallas, 1926) about the ways in which acts of creative thinking develop: early 'preparation' stages may be highly collaborative and social, with ideas discussed and tested out with others, but this may be followed by a more solitary 'incubation' stage, in which children take time to reflect and develop their own viewpoints (Claxton, 1999).

What are the implications for adult roles here? Perhaps most important is their sensitivity to children's ways of thinking and acting. Sometimes children may enjoy collaborating, with adults and/or with peers, whilst at other times they can find it more helpful to think and act alone, or to engage in different activities to those planned, and this may be more valuable than encouraging them to join in with others (Honig, 2001).

The physical environment: space, time and choice in young children's creative thinking

The physical environment reflects and supports the pedagogical vision of those working within it (Vecchi, 2010), and can impact upon what children do, and the relationships they make (Robson, 2009a). Vygotsky (2004: 66) stresses that 'the best stimulus of creativity in children is to organise their life and environment so that it leads to the need and ability to create'. This will be supported by opportunities for children to explore and engage in activities of their own choosing, and to imagine, hypothesize and speculate, in an atmosphere that values risk taking and ensures that children have enough time to complete activities. Eckhoff and Urbach (2008) argue that the close relationship between imagination and cognition makes it important that adults create an environment that incorporates opportunities for imagination, in which young children's creative thought and confidence are fostered. A rich example of this is provided by Burnard et al. (2006) in their description of a class of 4- and 5-year-old children, the teacher and teaching assistant, developing an interactive classroom display, reflecting ongoing activity and the children's questions, ideas and strategies as they engage in 'possibility thinking'.

These principles apply both indoors and outside. Outdoors can afford children time and space to think creatively (Robson and Hargreaves, 2005), and may influence the ways in which children play with materials (Broadhead, 2004), including generating a greater range of creative responses from them (Compton et al., 2010). The nature of the materials themselves may also be important. Lloyd and Howe (2003) found that, with the 4–5-year-old children in their research, open-ended materials were significantly positively associated with both intended and non-intended (novel, unusual) use, whereas closed-ended materials were only significantly associated with intended use, with less evidence of children's divergent thinking. Broadhead, with a similar age group, found that open-ended, non-representational resources, such as pieces of fabric, empty boxes and pieces of wood, supported highly social and cooperative activity amongst the children, as they speculated about, discussed and negotiated what these materials were to become. In so doing, the children were engaging in divergent thinking and problem solving. However, it is also worth bearing in mind that Lloyd and Howe (2003) also found that, for some children, particularly the solitary, active players, closed materials often stimulated more imaginative, divergent thinking.

Opportunities for children to exercise choice, both in the activity itself, and in the time they give to it, are important parts of these processes. Children's self-initiated play activities may often provide the strongest contexts for problem solving and extending their thinking (Lambert, 2000; Siraj-Blatchford et al., 2002).Wright (2010) highlights the ways in which the attitudes of significant adults can either encourage or inhibit children's creative thinking, dependent upon their openness to support the children's own ideas. Alongside this, children's understanding that they will be able to persist with an activity, and see it through to a satisfying conclusion, may influence what they choose to do. Giving sufficient, uninterrupted, time to children's problem solving supports the development of deeper understanding and more complex knowledge (Lambert, 2000). Claxton (2006) suggests that adults should make time for 'reverie' in children – opportunities for them to spend quiet time reflecting on what they are about to do – as supportive of creative learning.

Creative thinking and young children's play

How might young children's creative thinking be supported by their play? In many ways this question is addressed throughout the book, but it is valuable to look more closely at the centrality of play for young children, and its relationship to creative thinking. The Early Years Foundation Stage in England emphasizes that 'Play underpins all development and learning for young children ... and it is through play that they develop intellectually, creatively, physically, socially and emotionally' (DfES, 2007: 7). Similar emphasis is evident in early childhood curricula across the world (see, e.g. OECD, 2004). Prentice (2000) draws attention to the close relationship between young children's play and imaginative activity, and for Vygotsky (2004), children's play is the creative reworking of their impressions, not merely a reproduction of their experiences. In particular, we would emphasize the importance of playfulness as supportive of creativity, and a conception of play as attitudinal, an approach to action rather than any specific activity (Bruner, 1977).

The taxonomy of play outlined by Hutt (1979) and Hutt, Tyler, Hutt and Christopherson (1989) provides a valuable parallel with aspects of both creative and critical thinking. This taxonomy identifies epistemic and ludic behaviour as the two chief aspects of young children's play. Epistemic behaviour is concerned with the acquisition of knowledge, information and skills (Hutt et al., 1989). It may involve exploration and problem solving, and is particularly characteristic of playing with something new, and exploring ideas of 'What can it do?'. Ludic behaviour, by contrast, is 'essentially diversive, that is, concerned with self-amusement' (Hutt et al., 1989: 222) and related to playing for the fun of it. The two major categories of ludic behaviour are symbolic, or fantasy play, involving representation and pretence, and repetitive play, involving the rehearsal of skills and concepts already acquired. It is characterized by more of a sense of mastery and exploring ideas of 'What can I do with it?'.

At first glance, it would be easy to identify the characteristics of epistemic behaviour as reflecting qualities associated with critical thinking, and ludic behaviour as more clearly reflecting creative thinking. However, as we have already suggested in Chapter 2, these distinctions may inaccurately reflect the extent to which creative thinking in young children's play operates alongside critical thinking, with children moving in and out of these two modes of thinking. Presented with a new idea, or novel material, for example, children's first actions may be to explore and investigate it, to find out what it can do. Having explored its properties, children may feel more at ease, and more confident about trying out new, divergent ideas for the material. Craft (2001) identifies this process of movement from 'What can it do?' to 'What can I do with it?' as at the heart of what she describes as 'possibility thinking', a significant dimension of creative learning. This process may, in addition, be cyclical, as children try out ideas, and return to them, with deeper understanding, reflecting Vygotsky's (2004) view of the relationship between imagination (generally reflected in ludic activity) and reality (more characteristic of epistemic behaviour). In both cases, young children's critical and creative thinking capabilities are working together to find solutions to the problems they set for themselves. The same may also be true of problems set for them by others. Sylva, Bruner and Genova (1976) demonstrated that, in a problem-solving activity, a group of children who were given opportunities to play freely with materials and create their own approaches and solutions subsequently out-performed another group who were 'taught' how to use the materials in ways which would help them to solve a given problem. Furthermore, the group that had the experience of play showed more evidence of creative thinking, being both more inventive and creative in the strategies they used, and more persistent in their attempts to solve the problem.

The importance of pretence

Pretend play exemplifies Vygotsky's (2004) description of creative activity as the use of recalled experiences to imagine something new, and to innovate. As such, young children's engagement with pretence of all kinds may be particularly valuable both for encouraging the development and expression of creative thinking, and in providing opportunities for practitioners and researchers to see it occurring. Singer (1973) concurs, viewing pretend play and make-believe of all kinds as facilitatory for creative and flexible thinking. Looking at the ACCT framework categories, pretend play is often something in which young children choose to engage, with clear ideas of what they want to do. Framing play scenarios, making objects, resources and places stand for something else, taking on roles, and engaging in pretend communication all require participants to think flexibly, imagine and try out ideas, analyse and speculate, and generate new ideas and solutions. In socio-dramatic play this will be a collaborative activity, with participants further hypothesizing about other people's wishes and intentions, as they negotiate story lines and characters, and imagine how co-players will feel, think and act.

Communication and language

Siraj-Blatchford (2007) identifies communication, creativity and collaboration as a triumvirate of interactive principles central to high quality early childhood practice. For Wegerif (2010), the metaphor of thinking as dialogue is central to creative thinking, echoing Hobson's (2002) ideas about the dialogic bond between caregiver and baby, as each seeks to see things from the other's perspective. When children move into settings, this dialogic relationship is just as important. Sylva et al. (2010) found, for example, that sustained shared thinking was most likely to occur in conversations between children and adults (particularly one-to-one conversations), in which there was a shared focus on children's activities. Educators in Reggio Emilia (Project Zero/Reggio Children, 2001) suggest that young children's thinking is a collective process, dependent upon discussion and 'provocation' to challenge existing theories and ideas. In this discursive process, adults and children play equally vital parts, and Mercer's (2000) accounts of children talking together illustrate that children can effectively support one another in developing their creative thinking.

Wegerif (2010) emphasizes the benefits of creating an atmosphere of genuine dialogue between children and adults, in which talking about thinking is actively pursued. In the FRF project, some of the most effective practitioners showed this in their interactions with children, including using vocabulary such as 'think', 'remember', 'wonder' and 'know', and stimulating the children to reflect on past events. For the children themselves, the chance to talk about and reflect on an activity gave them opportunities to articulate their knowledge about their ideas, thoughts and feelings, more explicitly and in more detail than engaging in the activity itself (Robson, 2010).

In much the same way that we earlier emphasized the value of open-ended activities for young children's creative thinking, open-ended questioning by adults may stimulate children's thinking and help them to reflect upon it, and to make connections between their experiences (Wegerif, 2010). In the context of sustained shared thinking, Siraj-Blatchford et al. (2002: 47) suggest that adult interventions in the most effective settings in their study 'were most often in the form of questions that provoke speculation and extend the imagination'. Craft's notion of 'possibility thinking' (2001), with its stress on the idea of 'what if ...?' questions for developing creativity, emphasizes children's own questions as a part of this process, through the ways in which this can encourage children's imaginative, playful thinking. Wegerif (2010) sees this playful thinking as being facilitated by validation of playful talk. Often viewed by adults as 'off-task', he sees such talk as contributing to children's imagination and divergent thinking, as well as contributing to 'more obviously productive classroom talk' (Wegerif, 2010: 39).

To sum up, it will be important for adults working with young children to ensure that they engage in genuine dialogue with children, modelling appropriate language and strategies (Siraj-Blatchford, 2007) and open-ended questioning and reasoning (Wegerif, 2010). Helping children to make meaningful connections between ideas (Craft et al., 2008b), encouraging children's own questions and valuing playful talk will all support the development of creative thinking.

Conclusion

Looking at young children's creative thinking is simultaneously both simple and complex. As a universal capability, it can be seen in their every-day, familiar activities, as they play and talk with one another and with adults. At the same time, this means that the potential for adults to both observe and support its development are complex and wide ranging, across all aspects of young children's experience and in all kinds of physical and affective contexts.

In this chapter we have focused on the messages of research, theory and practice in considering how young children's creative thinking may develop, and how adults can potentially observe and support it in early childhood settings. Whilst a range of cultural, social and situational contexts are here considered separately, they work together to create an environment in which young children can display and develop their creative thinking. The centrality of play and talk are as significant for creative thinking as they are for other aspects of young children's development, and opportunities for children to engage freely in self-initiated play activities and playful talk and interaction are vital. The implications for practitioners are clear, pointing to the fostering of a supportive atmosphere in which children's own ideas, engagement, risk taking and persistence are valued, and in which reflecting on their own thinking is an everyday activity.

〜〜 Reflection

- Think about yourself when faced with a novel situation – how do you respond? Look at Claxton's (1999) model of processes in the development of acts of creative thinking (preparation, incubation, illumination and verification) and the Hutt (1979; Hutt et al., 1989) Play Taxonomy – are there any similarities between your behaviour and their ideas?

- What are your views on Sternberg's assertion that 'creative people are creative, in large part, because they have *decided* to be creative' (2003: 333)?

- Think of some spaces for young children with which you are familiar – homes, outdoor play spaces, nurseries, schools, day-centres, crèches. What would you identify in any of these spaces as particularly facilitating young children's creative thinking? Are there aspects of any of these spaces which you think can militate against young children's attempts to think creatively?

Social relationships in early childhood

Hiroko Fumoto and Sue Greenfield

This chapter focuses on:

- The social and cultural contexts of children's creative thinking and 'cultural contextualism' (Kağitçibaşi, 2007);

- The social and cultural nature of children's creative thinking and the ways in which social relationships are ingrained in the development of children's thinking;

- The communicative relationships that develop between children, parents and teachers, and their role in understanding and promoting children's creative thinking.

As Chapters 2 and 3 have highlighted, positive social relationships in early childhood are likely to be critical in promoting children's creative thinking. Over the years, the significance of social relationships on children's learning and development has been demonstrated in a number of studies. For instance, several studies have been conducted to explore various aspects of mother–child (e.g. Kochanska et al., 2009) and teacher–child relationships (e.g. Fumoto et al., 2007; Howes et al., 2008). Increasingly, there are studies of father–child relationships (e.g. Dunn et al., 2004; Shears, 2007) and the roles grandparents play in children's lives (e.g. Kenner et al., 2007). Studies on peer and sibling relationships have also been invaluable in understanding the developmental contexts of children's development (e.g. Pike et al., 2005). In addition, there is a growing body of literature on parent–teacher relationships (e.g. Mendez, 2010; Reedy and McGrath, 2010). What these studies demonstrate is the interrelatedness of each relationship and its significant bearing on children's well-being. For example, positive teacher–child relationships can facilitate children's relationships with their peers (e.g. Shin, 2010) and can also compensate for children who are 'less securely attached' with their mothers (e.g. Buyse et al., 2011: 33).

By building on the discussion in the preceding chapters, this chapter focuses on social and cultural dimensions of young children's creative thinking. As Glăveanu (2010: 80) suggests, we also see creativity as 'a fundamentally relational, intersubjective phenomenon'. What does this mean, and what might be the implications for parenting and for early childhood practice? Given the importance of social relationships in early childhood, this chapter examines their link with children's creative thinking.

Social and cultural contexts of creative thinking: cultural contextualism

The premise of our discussion rests on the idea of 'cultural contextualism', which refers to the ways in which culture serves as 'context in the study of psychological phenomena' (Kağitçibaşi, 2007: 370). Clearly, creative thinking and social relationships are both psychological phenomena that are embedded in social and cultural contexts, although 'culture' itself is still a much debated concept (e.g. Matsumoto, 2006). In this chapter, we refer to culture as 'social systems' (Derksen, 2007: 194) in line with Kağitçibaşi's (2007) conceptualization. As she suggests, culture can be seen as 'the context of psychological functioning' that gives 'meaning to observed behavior' and to 'their environments' (2007: 56). This way of considering culture illustrates how deeply it permeates children's development. It also resonates with theoretical perspectives such as Bronfenbrenner's (1979) ecological model of human development, and developmental systems theory (Ford and Lerner, 1992), which view individuals' development as ingrained in the context of their lives. This implies that creative thinking and social relationships can be seen as phenomena that are likely to change over time, whereby individuals influence the environment in which they are embedded through their 'self-organising and self-constructing' nature (Lerner, 2002: 184).

Surprisingly, the notion of culture in understanding children's creative thinking has been left relatively unexamined (Craft, 2008), with the exception of research on how different countries understand and promote creativity (e.g. Kaufman and Sternberg, 2006, 2010). In contrast, many authors have written about social contexts that are likely to promote children's creative thinking. For instance, the social context is often cited as facilitating security, which is based on a feeling of freedom from being judged, but at the same time providing stimulation and challenge (Craft, 2008; Duffy, 2009). Claxton,

Edwards and Scale-Constantinou (2006: 60) emphasize the significance of creating 'a climate that affords or even invites creative thinking, but one that stretches and thereby strengthens the creative habits and dispositions'. Kemple and Nissenberg (2000: 68) talk about a 'creative family environment' as consisting of 'respect for the child, stimulation of independence, and an enriched learning environment'.

According to Glăveanu (2010), the social context of creativity has not received sufficient attention until relatively recently. He explains that for many years, *'holistic and systemic ways'* of considering creativity have been neglected in individualized approaches in which attention has focused solely on people's cognitive function (2010: 83), to which we referred in Chapter 2. Glăveanu suggests that authors such as Amabile (1996) and Hennessey (2003), and their work on motivation, have promoted the social aspect of creativity in research. In particular, their focus on intrinsic motivation has had an important bearing on understanding the ways in which adults can support the development of children's creativity.

Our focus on the social and cultural contexts of children's creative thinking has helped us take a close look at two important issues that have been somewhat undermined in the discussion on creativity. The first is the significance of the family environment, and its links with children's experience in early childhood settings. Historically, the value of family environment, and especially the mother's influence on her children, has been acknowledged as playing an important part in developing early childhood practice, not only in countries in the west but also in the east. Undoubtedly, family environment is hugely important in every aspect of children's lives, as Kağitçibaşi (2007: 2) explains: '... the study of the person and human development automatically implicates the family as the context, and thus features the family explicitly in the conceptualization. Similarly, when the family is under focus, it is automatically situated in its sociocultural environment'. Her work indicates that family environment is not just an 'external factor' that influences children, but is embedded in their development as they internalize the family's values and attitudes: and this process, in turn, is influenced by children's own interpretation and temperament. As she notes: 'the family plays a key mediating role in the functional/causal relations between the self and society' (2007: 168).

This way of considering the family environment provides grounds for exploring the extent to which children's creative thinking is embedded in the socio-cultural context of such environment. Early childhood settings also reinforce and extend this context as they work towards supporting families. Despite the complexity of involving parents in research (see Chapter 6), there is a clear need to explore their perspectives when we investigate children's creative thinking, as we have done in the FRF project.

The second issue is the ways in which social and cultural contexts are understood in creativity research. Glăveanu (2010) suggests that one important distinction needs to be made in understanding the role these contexts play in creativity, namely, that between 'the social as an *external environment*' that promotes or inhibits children's creative thinking, and 'the social roots, social dynamics and social functions of creativity' (2010: 83). In essence, socio-cultural context not only serves to influence children's creative thinking from 'outside', but also involves 'the social and cultural working from *within* the creative person and process' (2010: 84). Glăveanu refers to the latter as a 'cultural psychology of creativity' (2010: 84) and distinguishes it from the former, which Amabile's (1996) work on the social psychology of creativity, amongst others, has promoted. For him, the former does not go far enough in understanding the ways in which social and cultural contexts influence creativity:

> ... the discussion of the social in her [Amabile's] book is constantly framed in terms of choice and constraints, reward, competition, modelling, stimulation, evaluation, peer pressure, surveillance, etc. and therefore does not abandon the understanding of creativity as an individual-level phenomenon 'conditioned' by social factors (Glăveanu, 2010: 83).

Glăveanu contends that these ways of considering social contexts limit them as 'an environment that has the power to facilitate or inhibit creative expression' (2010: 90) and that this is insufficient in understanding the influence that social relationships have on creativity. As he argues: '[i]n the end, the person still sits "alone", self-contained and self-sufficient, ready to confront the "system" and, if "creative enough", to defeat it' (2010: 90–1). Here, Glăveanu is not referring to the link between social relationships and creativity in a simple binary fashion, that is, in terms of the contrast between 'external' versus 'internal' influences. Children internalize 'what is out there' through cultural mediation, as Vygotsky's (1978) work indicates. Glăveanu also acknowledges this by emphasizing that 'the Vygotskyian perspective remains central to any cultural perspective on creativity' (2010: 85). His argument is that research on the cultural psychology of creativity that demonstrates the social and cultural nature of creative development is still scarce, and that this deserves fuller consideration.

Social relationships and creative thinking

Studies that explore the social and cultural contexts of children's development demonstrate how children develop their capacity to think through their relationships with others. For instance, as we saw in Chapter 3, Hobson (2002: 148) illustrates how 'thinking is not merely an individual affair', but that it emerges out of our relationships with significant others, especially those between mother and infant. An emotional engagement with the mother (i.e. the primary caregiver) enables infants to become aware of 'other people's engagement with the world' (Hobson, 2002: 142).

In other words, children come to develop their thinking through realization that other people have minds that are different to their own. For instance, gaze, and the facial and physical expressions of the mother indicate her thoughts about something. Her verbal communication can express her thoughts about herself and about the child. These interactions with the mother give rise to the ways in which infants develop their capacity to think, as they develop language (as a tool) and self-awareness, which are necessary when thinking about one's relationship with the outside world (Hobson, 2002).

This process of developing children's thinking demonstrates how deep-rooted social relationships are in children's development. According to Hobson (2002), it is not just the observable interactions between children and their significant others that influence children's thinking, but also 'someone else's emotional presence' that can 'strengthen or weaken an individual's capacity to think at all' (2002: 22). Glăveanu (2010: 86) refers to this as 'social-dialogical processes' and suggests that: '... even when we are alone and apparently creating in complete solitude, we are still engaged in dialogue with internalised 'parties' such as our mentors, our audience, our critics, etc.'. As Anthony Storr (1988: 16) writes in his seminal work *Solitude*, such social relationships can also build our 'capacity to be alone', which plays an important role in the ways children develop their creative thinking.

This also leads us to consider how the social and cultural nature of young children's creative thinking can result in particular ways of thinking. For instance, Kim's (2005) study compared the influence of East Asian and American education on children's creativity. Interestingly, an external environment such as an education system can mutually reinforce the relational patterns that have been identified in mother–child relationships research: studies of Japanese and western mother–child relationships are a case in point. According to Rothbaum et al. (2000), 'symbiotic harmony', which emphasizes the importance of accommodation (i.e. adapting oneself to others), is more likely to be observed in Japanese than in American mother–child relationships, and 'generative tension' based on individuation (i.e. tension between the desire to be close and the need to explore) is more likely to be shown in American than Japanese mother–child relationships. In Japan, emphasis is placed on promoting 'empathy, compliance and propriety', whereas American mother–child relationships appear to reinforce children's 'autonomy, expressiveness and exploration' (Rothbaum et al., 2000: 1122). The kind of relationships that American mothers promote are closely associated with important factors often identified as the basis of developing creative thinking, as referred to earlier, which are generally thought to be promoted in their education systems.

Inevitably, there are differences within any given culture and, with globalization, the cultural nature of education and social relationships are changing rapidly. Indeed, 'western' and 'eastern' characteristics are becoming increasingly fused. Yet, as Nisbett (2003: 77) suggests: 'the variations between and within societies, as well as within individuals, should not blind us to the fact that there are very real differences, substantial on the average, between East Asians and people of European culture'. In many ways, these studies provide an important way of looking at how culture can give rise to diverse ways of thinking, which are probably influenced by the patterns of relationships that are likely to emerge in a particular culture.

Communicative relationships and creative thinking at home and at school

What might be the implications of the links between creative thinking and social relationships for parenting and early childhood practice? In this section, we focus on the importance of the communicative relationships between parents, children and teachers that are underpinned by 'emotional connectedness' (Hobson, 2002). This includes spontaneous interactions initiated by children, and teachers' and parents' ease in tuning in to children's feelings (cf. Pianta, 2001). Furthermore, teachers' sensitivity towards parents' emotional states is also important, as the case studies in this chapter illustrate. In essence, communicative relationships involve adults' ability to listen to children's thoughts (Fumoto, 2011), and for teachers, this extends to their ability to understand the parents with whom they work.

 Case study: 1

> It is the first day of school. Rob, a 3-year-old, comes into the classroom clinging on to his mother. He sobs and holds on to her. The mother looks anxious and says to the teacher, Ms. Sheila: *'I'll stay for a while'.* Sheila replies: *'That's fine. We all went through this'* and smiles and puts her hand on the mother's shoulder to comfort her. Before long, the mother is ready to leave although Rob is still looking tense and worried. Sheila says to her in a comforting manner: *'I'll call you later to let you know how he is.'* She then kneels down and looks at Rob at his eye level and gives him a cuddle and then directs his attention to what other children are doing and asks him if he wants to join in. As the mother walks out of the classroom, she turns around to see Rob standing by other children holding Sheila's hand.

 Case study: 2

> In an interview, a mother of a 4-year-old talked about her child's teacher: *'She doesn't talk to children like they are "infants". She talks to them like they are human beings and understands what they are*

saying and I really appreciate that. I really appreciate the ways she understands children's different ways of thinking and different ways of asking questions'.

Case study: 3

Another mother talked about her son's teacher in a different setting: '*a couple of times when I dropped him off, the teacher was speaking to the children in a very harsh way. There were times when she was very angry at somebody. Her main goal seems to be to control the class when I feel that children need freedom to develop their thinking within some kind of boundaries'.*

In the first case study, what if Sheila did not recognize the parent's anxiety about leaving her child on the first day of the school? Even if she was aware of it, what might be the effect on the parent, and indeed on the child, if she failed to demonstrate her empathy and compassion?

What about the two mothers' experiences of their children's teachers in case studies 2 and 3? How would they be forming trusting relationships with the teachers? In what ways do these teachers affect the parents' confidence in leaving their children in their care? Might they feel that their children are valued, and that their creative thinking is being promoted?

Of particular importance in understanding the meaning of communicative relationships is Buber's (1878–1965) influential work on *I and Thou* (Buber, 1937). He argued extensively about the ways in which we distinguish our encounters with other individuals from the act of coming across some material objects. While the idea of 'I–Thou' stemmed from his theological work, Buber's identification of 'I–It' and 'I–Thou' relations indicates that perceptions of material objects ('It') are distinct from our perceptions of other individuals ('Thou'), in which the former is regarded as an '*object of our experience*' and the latter as '*a subject who is in communication with us*' (Crossley, 1996: 11). For Buber, a dialogue does not always indicate extensive exchanges of ideas and thoughts between individuals, but it does include exchanges of a glance and a smile between strangers. As he suggests (1937):

> I would rather think of something unpretentious yet significant – of the glances which strangers exchange in a busy street as they pass one another with unchanging pace. Some of these glances, though not charged with destiny, nevertheless reveal to one another two dialogical natures. (Buber, 1937: 5–6)

This extended view of dialogue demonstrates the importance of subtle non-verbal communication between children and adults in their mutual perceptions of each others' internal states (such as an intention and emotion). In analysing Buber's work, Morgan and Guilherme (2010) point out the importance of 'dialogical communities' in education, in which the process is based on the notion of 'an encounter of equals, who recognise each other as such' (2010: 4). This demonstrates the importance of how each one of us treats other people. In early childhood settings, the establishment of 'dialogical communities' can rely heavily on what, and how, teachers communicate with children and parents, and the ways in which different messages are received by them. The case studies in this chapter illustrate the subtlety of social relationships in early childhood settings, and reveal the importance of teachers' sensitivity towards parents and children.

Two practical points about young children's creative thinking emerge from this analysis. The first is that, at a most fundamental level, communicative relationships should form the basis of early childhood practice. The younger the children, the more adults may find it difficult to listen to their thoughts, as children may not have developed ways of fully communicating them. On the other hand, several studies demonstrate the sophisticated ways in which infants communicate with others (e.g. Gopnik, 2009; Grosse et al., 2010; Hobson, 2002). These studies emphasize the importance of practitioners and parents continuing to improve their skills and abilities so as to help them to tune into what young children are trying to communicate to them.

Communicative relationships between parents and teachers are also of great consequence in promoting children's creative thinking. For instance, Alasuutari's study (2009: 115) in Finland demonstrates how 'shared laughter' between parents and teachers helped to construct 'settings for negotiating potential interactional problems and produced affiliation, alignment and also intimacy'. Alasuutari (2009) suggests that shared laughter between parents and teachers seems to facilitate the communication between them. It is also noted that in Finland, the relationships between parents and teachers are fairly symmetrical rather than asymmetrical, indicating equality and partnership between them. Such a relationship is likely to promote the 'dialogical communities' referred to above. This seems important in creating an environment where not only the children, but also the parents and the teachers, can enhance the ways in which they make 'decisions' that underlie creative thinking (Sternberg, 2003): this issue was discussed in Chapter 3.

Secondly, when we talk about *children's* creative thinking, we need to be aware that its expression can be very diverse and can develop in multiple ways, as our earlier discussion indicates. The notion of cultural contextualism (Kağitçibaşi, 2007) implies that communicative relationships between children, parents and teachers are central in understanding this diversity. The contexts that we take for granted when communicating with someone from a similar background may not be familiar to others from different social and cultural backgrounds. It is likely that children internalize their contexts of development (including their social relationships) in multifaceted ways, and this must be recognized when examining children's creative thinking.

Li et al.'s (2010) study illustrates the point. They explored the ways in which 4-year-olds express their understanding of the purpose of 'school learnings' in the United States, and found significant differences between children from different cultural and socio-economic backgrounds. Chinese children from a middle-class background mentioned the significance of 'adult expectation and seriousness of learning', whereas their European-American counterparts reported 'positive affect for self and compliance with adults' as important. Their responses seem to reflect the ways in which Chinese culture tends to see learning as 'not conceptualized as a process driven by children's fluctuating interest, curiosity, and fun, but by commitment and willingness to overcome difficulties and hardships' (Li et al., 2010: 1647). In contrast, European and American cultures tend to value aspects such as intrinsic motivation, self-expression, curiosity and personal interest, which are often seen as essential in promoting creative thinking. Also, whereas western countries may focus on listening to children, there appears to be an emphasis for Chinese children on 'listenership in communication' (2010: 1638). Li et al. explain that this is possibly because:

> ... learning to self-perfect requires much contemplation, self-examination, and daily personal exertion. A person who can talk well may not take action toward achieving learning goals. Hence, Chinese culture stresses what children *do* to learn but not what they *say* they will do to learn. (2010: 1638)

Again, as Li et al. (2010) acknowledge, the differentiation between western and eastern cultures, and Chinese and European American cultures, is a crude way of looking at possible cultural differences (and similarities). Factors such as family environment and socio-economic status also play a significant role in determining how children develop their attitudes towards learning. Aspects such as child-initiated activities and enjoyment in learning also seem to be increasingly valued by Chinese parents and teachers. However, Li et al.'s (2010) study indicates how the social and cultural contexts that children experience at home and at school, and in particular the adults' expectations towards children's learning, are internalized by the children. These processes of socialization and enculturation are likely to have a profound impact on the ways in which children develop and express their creative thinking. This in turn, presents teachers with the challenge to understand such processes by developing communicative relationships with children and their parents.

Conclusion

The discussion in this chapter suggests that when exploring children's creative thinking, there is a strong need to be open-minded about the ways in which they express their creative thinking and how each family supports this process. Cultural contextualism provides us with useful ways of questioning our own assumptions about what creative thinking should 'look like', and helps us to take into consideration the cultural and social contexts as essential factors in understanding this process. It also calls for early childhood practitioners' sensitivity towards and awareness of the diverse ways in which children express their creative thinking, and the cultural and social nature of creativity itself. In addition, the ways in which practitioners treat parents and children can go a long way in ensuring communication that can set the tone of the social contexts that develop in early childhood settings.

The discussion also raises many wider issues. For instance, consideration of the social and cultural nature of children's thinking can easily slip into cultural relativism in which 'every act is assumed to have a unique meaning deriving from its specific context' (Kağitçibaşi, 2007: 8). As Kağitçibaşi asserts, this is not helpful in understanding children's lives and their development. There are aspects that can be generalized across cultures and there are aspects that are culturally specific, depending on circumstances and individuals. It is important to take into consideration the ways in which social and cultural contexts may influence the development of children's creative thinking rather than simply looking for differences and interpreting them all as 'cultural differences'.

We also believe that the exploration of children's creative thinking should happen within the spirit of 'communicative dialogue', based on the notion of communicative relationships discussed in this chapter. This is particularly important since the field has been dominated by authors from Europe and North America. A student from Asia who was studying at a university in England once said: 'I feel that the education I had in my home country was backward because it wasn't child-centred at all' (personal communication). We need to be cautious when emphasizing what constitutes pedagogy that promotes children's creativity. As we have discussed, there are many diverse ways in which children learn and engage with their environments, and an emphasis on pedagogy alone can undermine what they themselves bring to nurturing their own creative thinking. Further exploration of social relationships and creative thinking can help us understand the subtle and diverse ways in which children express their creative thinking, and the multiple ways in which adults around them support this process.

Reflection

- In what ways do you feel that the social and cultural contexts that you have experienced have affected the ways you express your creative thinking?

- What might be the similarities and differences between your own experience and that of someone from a different cultural background?

- If you are a practitioner, think about children in your early childhood settings, and discuss the different ways in which each child expresses his/her creative thinking.

- If you are a practitioner, think about parents in your early childhood settings, and discuss the ways in which they express their expectations of children's learning. If there are differences between the aims of the settings and the parents' expectations, how could you reconcile them?

- As a researcher, how would you incorporate the social and cultural contexts of children's creative thinking in your data analysis?

Part 2

Exploring Perspectives in Early Childhood Research

The second part of the book has three chapters which deal with the methodological issues of investigating children's, parents' and practitioners' experiences respectively. These are dealt with separately in each chapter in order to highlight some of the issues that are particularly relevant to each group, although other issues, such as the ways in which participants should be respected in the process of research, apply to all.

In Chapter 5, Sue Robson starts by asking why we talk about conducting research *with* children rather than '*on* or *about*' them: this is an important question that underpins the discussion in all chapters. She illustrates some of the exciting ways in which children's creative thinking can be explored with them, and discusses the ethical issues that should be considered in this process. The participation of children in research has perhaps been one of the most significant developments in the field of early childhood and Robson, through her research on exploring children's thinking, examines the complexity of eliciting children's perspectives.

The focus of Chapter 6 is on research with parents. Sue Greenfield uses her work with parents to raise and illustrate some important questions about the implications of the diversity of the different families participating in research studies. One important aspect of conducting research is that we should try our best to understand the participants' particular circumstances, and find ways of building trusting relationships with them. This chapter raises questions about the meaning of 'partnership' with parents in research and in early childhood practice, which is widely seen as being very important in promoting children's creative thinking.

In Chapter 7, Hiroko Fumoto considers the notion of researchers and practitioners collaborating on research. This chapter draws on the ongoing debate about mixed methods research and its emphasis on intersubjectivity, which places social relationships at the heart of the research enterprise. It also addresses the tension that still exists between using quantitative and qualitative approaches in exploring children's learning and development. In our work with undergraduate and postgraduate students, we come across many who are set on 'measuring' children's development without fully grasping the need to interpret the data in relation to the complexity of children's lives. On the other hand, there are also many students who resist quantitative approaches from the start, on the basis of their firm belief that statistical analysis conflicts with the ways in which they want to understand children's lives. The chapter attempts to ease this tension so that we can take advantage of both approaches.

5

Children's voices: young children as participants in research

Sue Robson

This chapter focuses on:

- The importance of children's perspectives on their lives, and the growth of interest in research with children;

- The value of children's perspectives about their creative thinking;

- Ethical and practical questions about research with children, particularly the use of video data and reflective dialogue with young children;

- How approaches to research with children are also valuable tools for practitioners in supporting the development of young children's creative thinking.

Why do we talk about research *with* children?

In recent years there has been a considerable shift of emphasis away from ideas of research *on* or *about* children, to research *with* children, underpinned by the belief that young children have much of value to say about their lives, and can be competent research participants, with the right to be treated as such (Christensen and James, 2008). The rationale for eliciting children's perspectives has arisen from several sources, including the sociology of childhood research movement, exemplified by the work of

James and Prout (1997), and the Children's Rights movement, recognized in the United Nations' *Convention on the Rights of the Child* (United Nations, 1989). This right to freedom of expression, particularly for young children, is emphasized in the more recent United Nations General Comment No. 7 (OHCHR, 2005), including, with regard to research, in the development of policies and services.

At the same time, there are tensions between children's rights of participation and their rights to protection (Schiller and Einarsdottir, 2009). Clark and Moss (2001) emphasize the importance of respecting children's privacy, and of bearing in mind that adult 'listening' is not a right. Broström (2005, cited in Einarsdottir, 2007) asks whether it is even in children's best interests that adults uncover details of their lives, suggesting that their rights to privacy and protection are a more important priority. It is valuable to keep these issues in mind whilst reading this chapter.

Approaches to research with children

Research with children poses ethical, methodological and practical questions and challenges. Methodologically, a range of imaginative and thoughtful approaches have been developed, for example, using stories, oral and written journals, drawing (Dockett and Perry, 2005), role play (Cousins, 1999), photography (Smith et al., 2005) and the Mosaic approach of Clark and Moss (2001). All of these are well documented in the original sources. In this chapter, the focus is on two particular tools for eliciting children's perspectives: the use of video data, and reflective dialogues (RD), employed extensively in the FRF project. RD, a term coined by Moyles et al. (2002), is a technique used for discussions between researchers and practitioners. In the FRF project, the approach is used for discussions between adults and children. Excerpts of researcher-recorded video data of children's self-initiated activities are used as starting points for RD between child and practitioner, with a focus on what the child was doing and thinking during the activity. These two tools may be especially appropriate when the focus is on children's thinking, particularly when used in conjunction with one another, because they afford opportunities to focus both on what children actually do and on their reflections about their thoughts, feelings and actions. The video data and RD both function as semiotic tools (Vygotsky, 1978) in support of young children's thinking, supporting children's meaning-making.

Using camcorders and video data

The use of video recorders as tools in research began in the fields of social and visual anthropology and ethnography, and is now widespread across the social sciences. It is increasingly popular in research which focuses on participatory approaches. However, in relation to young children, it has often been used for the purposes of practitioner reflection (e.g. Moyles et al., 2002), or for analysis of the video data itself. With some exceptions (e.g. Forman, 1999; Morgan, A., 2007), less emphasis has been placed on the children's own perspectives and interpretations.

What, then, makes the use of video data, and in particular the children's own reflections on it, so valuable in the context of creative thinking? First, video itself may be helpful in research with children, given their interest in image-making of all kinds. The 'image-saturated everyday lives' (Thomson, 2008: 11) of many children means that they are highly practised in interpreting and making meaning from television and video images. Forman (1999) suggests that one of the benefits of using video data is that it can act as a 'tool of the mind', allowing children to 'download' details of their actions as part of replaying the video, freeing their minds to think about what those actions mean: 'Their knowledge that I was recording gave the children a reason to consider what in the classroom or in their own play was interesting' (Forman, 1999: 5). This, as he points out, demands high-level thinking on the part of the children.

Playing back video data can help both adults and children to recall context, and is multimodal – carrying evidence of action, body language, facial expression, and verbal interaction, in a linear narrative form. The possibility of replaying data over and over again, to different participants, supports discussion and collaborative reflection, richer and more diverse interpretations, and the potential for intersubjectivity and collaborative meaning making, as illustrated in the case study on intersubjectivity included here.

 Case study: Intersubjectivity and collaborative meaning-making

An extract from the RD between Tom (age 4.2) and James, his key person, as they watch a video episode of Tom riding a trike outdoors:

James: What are you asking Katie?

Tom: *Push* me up.

James: To *push* you up there, ah ....

Tom: It's ... and I done that.

James: You're asking her to push you. Well that was a good idea wasn't it? Because the trolley's very heavy isn't it? So if you get

(Continues)

> *(Continued)*
>
>   [someone to …·
>
> Tom: [Well no when I *check*ed it it's not very heavy for me.
>
> James: Oh, right. What when there's no one in the back it's not very heavy? Oh I see. But when there's someone in the back ….
>
> Tom: Yeah.

Thomson (2008, citing Freedman 2003) highlights how images elicit emotional and aesthetic responses as much as intellectual ones, with the potential for drawing out different responses to research which is primarily language-based. Anderson (cited in Bickham et al., 2001) has demonstrated that children pay closest attention to, and have strongest recall of, the television images which they comprehend best. It seems reasonable to infer that images of themselves and their actions fit such a criterion, so that using them to stimulate children's reflections ought to be fruitful. In addition, video recordings of children's own activities are set in contexts which have meaning for them. Children in the FRF research often showed excellent recall and knowledge, which included comments about themselves, for example Daniel (age 4.6) observing: 'Hey I'm not wearing them shoes today, I'm wearing shoelaces'; and appraisals of their own actions and those of others, for example Rachel's (age 4.7) observations of other participants in the activity she and her key person were watching:

> Rachel: (looking at screen, children playing with large construction materials, outdoors) Rebecca's spoiling it. That's Jasmin, that's Harry. Jakie's ruining it as well. I'm not. I asked Harry if we needed string, yeah, but Harry said no. I had a good idea. Move them along, yeah, then they can play fine whatever they wanna do with it, and they can break it.

It is also vital to remember that these processes are not neutral. Video data is produced or 'constructed' (Dahlberg et al., 2007) in a collaborative, mutually influencing process involving all participants (Banks, 2001). As Mondada (2009) suggests, participants observe and seek to interpret the actions and focus of the camera operator, inferring possible topics of interest on the operator's part, making the process highly interpretative and subjective.

Reflective dialogue

In seeking to elicit children's perspectives, attention to how they communicate their thoughts and feelings will have a central role. A social constructivist approach to children's thinking emphasizes that language is a tool for self-regulation (Vygotsky, 1986), and suggests the value of talk as a key way for children to both express and develop their thoughts. Vygotsky sees the development of thinking as proceeding from the social to the individual, making shared talk especially valuable for children's developing thinking. For Froebel, language 'is the expression of the human mind' (1888: 212), and a way of representing people's inner and outer worlds. Pramling (1988) demonstrates how explicit talk about learning and thinking may help to make young children more consciously aware of their thinking. However, A. Morgan (2007), observing children aged 3–7 years in school, concluded that children's perspectives were not valued, with them having few opportunities to talk about how they learnt, or reflected on their thinking – a view which is supported by Woodhead and Faulkner (2008). Siraj-Blatchford et al.'s study (2002) revealed that only a low proportion of the interactions they observed between adults and children were supportive of developing sustained shared thinking as compared with those which involved adults in direct teaching or monitoring.

It may be that valuable opportunities are potentially being lost, and that adults should pay closer attention to what children say about their thinking and learning, and make more effort to elicit ideas, and to provide 'provocation' (Project Zero/Reggio Children, 2001) to their existing ideas: this should be valuable both for gaining a deeper understanding of children's creative thinking, and for supporting its development. In the FRF project, when video material was played back to the children during the RDs, they would often spontaneously recount what they remembered they had been saying, sometimes weeks later, providing valuable evidence of their ability to recall past events and think abstractly. In one RD, whilst watching the video, Harry (age 4.10) playfully asked his key person, 'Guess what I'm doing!'. The discussions afforded children opportunities to display their knowledge, often in ways which might otherwise have remained invisible to the adults. Importantly, this supports the pedagogical value of video reflection, for teaching and learning as well as research.

The rest of this chapter considers some of the ethical and practical questions in research with children. Whilst these need to be addressed in all research with young children, the implications of using video are highlighted.

Who decides on the participants?

Whilst the intentions of researchers working with children may be that they should be active participants (Alderson, 2005), decisions about which children will be involved in a project rest first of all with adult gatekeepers: headteachers, managers, practitioners, parents and carers. Their consent is often sought before children are involved. So, for all adult groups, the emphasis is on opting *in* to a project. This raises an initial question: are there children who may want to be involved but cannot, because their parents do not opt in, for example, through lack of confidence or time? Conversely, it is not always possible to know whether any parents give consent out of a sense of obligation, fearing that, if they decline, relationships with the settings might be compromised.

Crucially, some parents may consent to their children's participation whilst the children themselves are more reluctant. Adult directions which are framed as 'requests' are often features of children's lives. For example, the expected response to 'Do you want to come and read with me now?' is not 'No' from a child, and it may be challenging for children to distinguish between these disguised imperatives and occasions when they truly have freedom of choice. The 'power dynamics of age' (Mauthner, 1997: 19) influence the relationships between children and adults more generally, and, along with relationships between researcher and 'researched', this may mean that young children are doubly disadvantaged (Christensen, 2004). Drawing on Foucault, Dahlberg et al. identify 'local settings' (2007: 35), such as early childhood institutions, as sites for the exercise of such disciplinary power. For all children, the result is that, unlike adults, they may only be able to signal their views effectively by opting *out*, rather than positively opting *in*, at the start of a project. This also highlights a paradox at the heart of research with children. As discussed earlier, current thinking positions children as social agents, with decision-making rights. At the same time they are also seen as being dependent on adults as intermediaries where research is concerned (Gallagher et al., 2010).

What do we mean by consent, and how can children's consent be sought?

The idea that all those involved in research should give their consent to participate has general acceptance globally. How this permission is established varies across countries, partly as a result of beliefs about children's development, with some suggestions that children under the age of 14 may not be competent to give consent (Bray, 2007), but also because of the legal status of participants' views. Under English law, competent minors can give consent, with competence being defined as having sufficient understanding and intelligence to understand the proposed project (Alderson and Morrow, 2004). By contrast, in Singapore and Australia the legal ages of consent are 21 and 18 respectively (Conroy and Harcourt, 2009). As a result, Conroy and Harcourt argue for use of the term 'assent' rather than 'consent'. In practice, and in the literature, assent and consent are often used interchangeably (Bray, 2007), and, as Gibson and Twycross (2007) point out, in a UK context at least, the legal difference remains unclear. Here, we use the term consent explicitly, as a way of affirming young children's competence to engage in 'the invisible act of evaluating information and making a decision, and the visible act of signifying the decision' (Alderson and Morrow, 2004: 96). Thus, as Smith et al. (2005) suggest, experience may be more important than age in discussions of consent.

How can children's consent be 'informed'?

The UNCRC (United Nations, 1989) asserts children's rights to seek, receive and impart information and express their views on all matters that affect them. Central to this, however, must be the extent to which children are able to make sense of and understand that information in order to ensure that they are fully informed. The British Educational Research Association (BERA)'s Revised Ethical Guidelines, for example, emphasize that 'children should ... be facilitated to give fully informed consent before research begins' (BERA, 2004: 7). Some imaginative approaches have been developed to support this facilitation, including tape-recorded explanations (Hill, 2005), opportunities for children to think about the research and consult with others (Dockett and Perry, 2007), illustrated information leaflets (Alderson, 2004), an 'activity board' (Bray, 2007), and, in the context of video data, showing potential participants video already produced as a way of supporting their understanding (Banks, 2001). However, the appearance of such material is not neutral, and carries messages about the positioning of children and the purposes of research which children may read in particular ways (David et al., 2001). Decisions also need to be made about what is enough information, and what might be too much, and thus potentially confusing for young children (Dockett and Perry, 2007).

There is a tension that is particular to video recordings, and, to a lesser extent, photographs. As stated above, the BERA Guidelines (2004) emphasize the importance of facilitating children's informed consent before beginning research. In the case of video data, it is arguable that part of that facilitation should include opportunities for children to see themselves on video, and reflect on how that feels for them, before giving their consent. Logically, therefore, researchers need children's consent to record them before they can really provide such fully informed consent. In the FRF project, children had extended opportunities to experiment with camcorders before their consent was sought, to help support their informed understanding. As the use of camcorders becomes more embedded in everyday practice, this tension may also become less marked. As Alderson (2008) suggests, children act as researchers in their activities in settings, for example, collecting data about favourite foods and researching their surroundings, and the use of camcorders in such contexts may be helpful in giving them opportunities to consider their feelings about appearing in recordings.

Heath et al. (2007) suggest that consent should be seen as 'consent-as-ongo-ing-negotiation', which continues to be negotiated and revisited, with children's consent regularly reaffirmed. In this respect, camcorders are little different to any other tool, except that they may be physically more intrusive than, say, a notepad and pencil. With this in mind, it may be important to give undertakings that camcorders will not be taken into areas regarded as private, for example, where children's personal care is being attended to. This does leave a lot of open ground for continual negotiation. Trying to remain sensitive to children expressing their consent or dissent, not just by talking but also through body language, is challenging if you have one eye on a camcorder screen. There is also a tension between trying to remain unobtrusive in order not to disrupt everyday life in the setting, and children always being aware that they are being filmed, and so able to give their consent knowingly. Children are often keen to participate, wanting what they are doing to be recorded, and wanting to see it played back, as in Rachel's suggestion one afternoon when we were recording inside: 'If you want to carry on videoing you'll have to come outside with me now', a clear example of a statement which affirmed her desire to continue to 'opt in'.

Rachel's comment was also characteristic of a phenomenon common to all of the settings in the FRF project: where children were playing alone, they would more frequently seek to involve researchers during recording than when they were in a group. This could be by look or gesture, but was often through talk, and as part of the narrative of the play, for example, Rosie's (age 4.5) comment to the researcher as she was being filmed: 'Look, I've built a wall!'. Children will also clearly signify when their interest wanes. For example, Harun (age 4.1) effectively ended an RD with his key person, and clearly exercised his right to opt out, by saying 'Can we finish it? It's making my head go dizzy'.

What about anonymity and confidentiality?

Data collection using techniques such as questionnaires and observations makes it relatively easy to protect participants' anonymity and confidentiality, by altering names and other identifying features. Visual material of any kind, particularly video data, is more problematic. Settings can be recognizable, and children may wear distinctive school clothing. Participants themselves are recognizable, and often use names in conversation. In addition, participant children and adults will talk and play with children in the setting who are not part of the project. Trying to 'screen' these children out is challenging, and necessitates either seeking further permission, or editing. The use of video, then, demands particular actions on the part of researchers, and 'puts children at particular risk and renders parents and practitioners vulnerable to criticism, anxiety and self-doubt' (Flewitt, 2005: 558). In the FRF project, some children did not want their identity to be anonymized, often feeling pride in being recognized for themselves, and thus emphasizing the importance of their own identity. This, however, may be problematic if it leads to the unwitting identification of others. Kellett (2010) discusses use of middle names, or those of a favourite toy, as alternatives.

Flewitt suggests that, in making use of visual images, 'the researcher should reflect on the degree of visual detail that is relevant to the research claim' (2005: 559), and consider reducing pixel counts, 'fuzzing', or making drawings of images. Whilst this should certainly be an option, when the research relies upon aspects such as facial expression and direction of gaze to infer aspects of creative thinking, as in the FRF project, valuable data could potentially be lost. In addition, Banks (2001) suggests that such devices may invoke ideas of criminality in viewers. What may be most important is to work with participants to provide opportunities to view material and request alteration or deletion, as well as ensuring that all are regularly reminded of their rights of choice and veto. This assumes particular significance nowadays, given the central part the internet plays in people's lives, and the potential for misuse of data.

Linked to this is the possibility that participants' attitudes may change over time, and children may become unhappy about recordings of their younger selves being used. On completion of any research project, data is stored for a period of time, though guidelines vary with regard to how long that might be. In the UK, for example, there is no national consensus, and guidelines differ across institutions and funding bodies. Decisions about data storage, its potential re-use, and possible disposal, raise the question 'Who owns the video?' (A. Morgan, 2007: 223). Ownership, copyright and access to data are recognized in the UK as potentially 'hazy areas' (Polydoratou, 2009: 306) for academic and research staff. Traditionally, ethics policies have focused on the ownership of institutions and researchers. However, the moral right of all participants to share ownership of research data has assumed increasing importance in recent years. In the case of video material, parents may be particularly keen to have copies of their children's activities, which makes it impossible for researchers to guarantee that such material will not find its way into wider public domains. Consideration needs to be given to complex questions of shared ownership, rights associated with ownership and access, and how to ensure that all participants' rights and wishes are respected. For example, consent forms may need to make more explicit the responsibilities of participants, and solicit their agreement, with regard to such shared ownership.

How can researchers try to be aware of their impact on participants?

Researchers will always have an impact, just by intervening in participants' lives. In the context of research with young children, this has three distinct, but overlapping, aspects: first, the researcher's identity as an adult coming into the children's domain; second, the researcher's role in producing data, which is never neutral; and third, the effect of the researcher's choice of what data is shared with the children.

The identity of the researcher: how do children see this?

As someone usually introduced to children by other adults – their teacher, for example – researchers come with a set of expectations, and the children may see them as other 'teachers', or people with some kind of power. O'Kane (2008) identifies disparities of power and status as the biggest challenge for researchers working with children, although, as Dahlberg et al. (2007) point out, this is not a one-way relationship: children themselves exercise power, and have an impact on researchers' behaviour towards them. Mandell (1991) advocates the adoption of a 'least-adult role' with the children, with the researcher 'operating physically and metaphorically on the children's level in their social worlds' (Mayall, 2008: 110). Christensen, however, draws attention to what she regards as the danger of this looking like a 'dubious attempt to be a child' (Christensen, 2004: 174), which could easily be seen by the children as patronizing. It seems inescapable that children will see any adult researcher as an adult, and thus that Christensen's idea of presenting as 'an unusual type of adult' (2004: 174), continually trying to balance being recognized as *an* adult whilst avoiding preconceived ideas children may have about 'adulthood', may be most likely to be successful.

In the context of projects which use camcorders, it is important to acknowledge that the camera will inevitably be part of the researcher's identity for the children, and continue to exert an impact on relationships (Pink, 2007). For example, in the FRF, whilst watching an extract, Anju (age 4.0) asked her keyperson 'Where's Sue?' He replied that I had gone back to my work. Her firm response 'In *there*', pointing at the video, expressed the identity I had for her, as part of the video process.

The impact of the researcher in the production of data

Time spent collecting as much data as possible may be one way of attempting to minimize the impact of the researcher on children's behaviour. This may reduce the potential for children to behave uncharacteristically, and help to minimize unconscious researcher biases, for example, towards recording particular types of activities. It is hugely time consuming, however, and it is neither practical nor desirable to be recording constantly. Nevertheless, the more time that can be spent, the more opportunity there may be to develop richer relationships with children, conducive to enhanced intersubjectivity and reflexivity (Lahman, 2008).

How can data most meaningfully be shared with children?

It is perhaps the sharing of data which holds the most important challenge with respect to the impact of the researcher. In the case of video data, images are never neutral: they are literally and socially constructed (Thomson, 2008). As operator of the camcorder, the researcher sees 'with' the camera, rather than 'through' it (Mondada, 2009), and it will be their decision what to record, and what to leave out, including decisions about when an activity chosen for replaying begins and ends. This effectively conditions what extracts are selected for discussion, and represents a level of analysis taking place during recording which is not apparent on later viewing (Plowman and Stephen, 2008). In addition, the act of using the camcorder, whilst possibly unconscious on the part of the researcher, including decisions made 'on the move' about framing shots, and about positioning, has an impact on what is recorded, and on how it is then interpreted by viewers. In the FRF project, for example, we attempted to minimize the potential for unwittingly influencing participants' interpretations about the importance of an event by avoiding zooming in on activities.

Bourdieu's analysis that understanding a photograph 'means not only recovering the meanings which it *proclaims* ... it also means deciphering the surplus of meanings which it *betrays*' (1990: 7, original emphasis) holds true for video data as well. Children are practised interpreters of the semiotics of television, and may infer particular meaning from the researcher's decisions. They will also bring their past experiences and social and cultural understandings to this process (Thomson, 2008). Data presented to participants is inevitably from the researcher's point of view, and from frontal angles. Whilst this may act to engage the viewer (Rose, 2001), it may also have the effect of positioning the researcher as controller of both space and time (2001), thus reinforcing a position of power in the children's eyes.

What is the value of involving children in feedback and dissemination about research?

Provision of feedback to any research participants can be problematic for many reasons, including the researcher's lack of time and money to do so. However, if we are to value children's perspectives, it is important to try to ensure their participation in feedback and dissemination. Alderson (2008) asserts that children may be particularly interested in being involved in those aspects of research which have the potential to impact positively on their everyday lives. MacNaughton et al. link such early opportunities for young children's involvement with their later 'abilities, identities and well-being' (2007: 461). This suggests the importance of finding effective ways of ensuring that longer-term outcomes are shared with children, along with their involvement in the dissemination and implementation of findings. This is a challenge when participants are young children, given that many may have moved on to other settings within a fairly short time.

Conclusion

This chapter has considered how video can be a highly motivating research tool, and a valuable means of eliciting children's perspectives, different to other methods, and of particular benefit when looking at children's creative thinking. As a semiotic tool (Vygotsky, 1978), it provides a context for interaction between the researcher, the child and the video episode, with the potential for producing rich data for the purposes of research. However, it also has similar potential for providing contexts for interactions between the practitioners, the children and the video episodes for pedagogical purposes, reminding children and adults of their context, and acting as a valuable support and stimulus for the development of young children's thinking and learning. In addition, the use of video data for the purposes of both research and practice has the potential to influence all participants' views about what happens in settings, and to really impact upon change.

Reflective dialogue gives researchers and practitioners invaluable opportunities to elicit children's perspectives, and to listen to their thoughts, ideas and feelings more directly, in ways that just observing, crucial though this is, cannot do. It can also help practitioners and researchers to become more aware of children's competence and understanding. This is vital if we are to plan most effectively for young children's development. At the level of research, the outcomes of discussions in which children's voices are truly heard may influence policy makers and curriculum developers, whilst the outcomes of individual practitioners' discussions with children can influence their everyday interactions with young children, and their decision making about planning and provision.

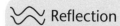 Reflection

Children's rights to express their views are enshrined in Article 12 of the UNCRC (United Nations, 1989):

> Parties shall assure to the child who is capable of forming his or her own views the right to express those views freely in all matters affecting the child, the views of the child being given due weight in accordance with the age and maturity of the child.

In research *with* children, attention to Article 13 is also important:

> The child shall have the right to freedom of expression; this right shall include freedom to seek, receive and impart information and

ideas of all kinds, regardless of frontiers, either orally, in writing or in print, in the form of art, or through any other media of the child's choice.

Reflect on what these Articles mean for you in practice:

- How do you know if a child is 'capable of forming his or her own views?'
- Can a commitment to listening to, and acting upon, the child's views be meaningfully fulfilled in care and education settings? Are some children's views listened to more than others? If so, why?

6

Involving parents in research

Sue Greenfield

> This chapter focuses on:
>
> - The diversity of parents and changing families, and the implications for involving them in research and in early childhood settings;
>
> - Parents' expectations of their children's learning;
>
> - Challenges in involving parents in research and in early childhood settings.

There is a current expectation that early childhood professionals will work 'in partnership' with parents (Morrow and Malin, 2004). The Children Acts (HMSO, 1989, 2004) highlight the importance of parental responsibility, and government policy in England has continued to stress the value of partnership with parents in health, education and social care (DCSF, 2008). Initiatives such as Sure Start and Children's Centres have also recognized the significance of parental involvement in children's learning and care, and the recent Tickell Review of the Early Years Foundation Stage (DfE, 2011) has further emphasized its importance. The value of parental involvement is also reinforced by the UK Effective Provision of Pre-school Education (EPPE) study (Sylva et al., 2010), which suggests that the most effective settings are those that share information between parents and staff. In these settings, parents are involved in their children's learning by negotiating learning programmes with practitioners and sharing educational aims. The EPPE study notes that this, in turn, enables parents to be engaged in their children's learning not only in the settings, but also at home.

Research shows that parental involvement is seen as important in expanding the social and cognitive capacities of children (Driessen et al., 2005). For instance, parents' levels of involvement are directly related to children's achievement at schools: the more they are involved, the higher their levels of achievement (Desforges and Abouchar, 2003). Parental involvement is seen to have a considerable effect on children's learning 'even after all other factors (such as social class, maternal education and poverty) have been taken out of the equation between children's aptitudes and their achievement' (Desforges and Abouchaar, 2003: 86). As Melhuish (2010: 67) stresses: 'The Home Learning Environment (HLE) in the pre-school period has association with all aspects of children's cognitive and social development and for much of a child's life is one of the most powerful influences upon development'. As suggested in the EPPE study, it is important that the emphasis should be placed on 'what parents do' rather than on 'who parents are'. The implication of this is that *all* parents have a vital role to play in children's learning, and that they should be supported by practitioners and other professionals who are involved in children's care and education.

Working with parents is not always easy, however, and much has been written about this (e.g. Crozier, 2001; Whalley and the Pen Green Centre Team, 2007). For instance, those practitioners who inadvertently take a 'school-centric' approach to parental involvement may fail to see things from the parent's perspective, making it difficult to develop a partnership that will support children's learning at home and at school (Lawson, 2003). It is also clear that not all parents wish to be involved (e.g. Brooker, 2002; Knopf and Swick, 2007). It is critically important that parents and practitioners respect and listen to each other in ways that accept alternative points of view.

The concept of parental involvement makes intuitive sense, as parents have the most in-depth knowledge of their individual children: few would disagree with this. However, if the understanding of this involvement is to be comprehensive, parents should also be involved in research, in order to provide a clearer perspective about family influences upon the ways in which children learn at home. When it comes to children's creative thinking, the topic of this book, little is known about the opportunities that parents provide. In order to develop the growing understanding of how children express their creative thinking in early childhood settings (Chapters 8, 10), it seems vital that research should involve parents, and should explore the ways in which they create the home environment with their children (e.g. Brown et al., 2009). However, it can be challenging for researchers to engender a trusting relationship with parents, especially with those who are unsure about taking part in research for a variety of reasons. Some of the points raised in Chapter 7 regarding the collaboration between practitioners and researchers are also relevant in promoting trust between parents and researchers.

The diversity of parents and families, and their involvement in research and in early childhood settings

The diversity of parents and families is often neglected in research and in early childhood practice. As discussed in Chapter 4, Bronfenbrenner's ecological systems theory (1979, 2005) has been helpful in enabling deeper discussion and understanding of parents and families. The theory provides an explanation for the uniqueness of each parent as a result of interactions between various factors such as culture, society, family, and their relationships with children and their own parents. A group of parents may at first seem a homogenous group, but when we consider the intricacies of ways in which these factors are interrelated, the diversity of parents and families become evident. All of these factors clearly influence family functioning, and determine the roles of parents in their children's lives and in their learning.

In addition, most of the views of early childhood settings developed in English-speaking countries are western rather than universal (Fleer, 2003; Rogoff, 2003). In research and early childhood practice, it is important to bear this in mind as we work increasingly with families from diverse communities. For example, Fleer (2003, 2008) discusses how, in some cultures, children do not always have special places designed for them with child-sized furniture and toys. Instead, they take part in the everyday life of the adult community, being involved with adults' day-to-day activities and helping where they can. Fleer describes this as the 'embeddedness of the child' within a community that shares responsibility for children, and which sees them as part of the adult world. In the Mayan communities, for instance, children learn by observation, often without verbal explanation of the activities from adults (Rogoff, 2003). This is in contrast to much early childhood practice and parenting in England in which verbal communication between children and adults is highly valued. Penn (2005) also provides a clear example of how ideas developed in the west are having an impact on early childhood practice in other countries. For example, Penn observed a setting in Africa where practitioners set up activities in the same way as they would in the west. They included a sand tray, as would be normal practice in the West, without reflecting that the children who attend are surrounded by sand all the time. They play outside, so a tray provides a much more limited experience for them.

Also, children's development may be viewed from a western perspective by many practitioners in England (Brooker, 2002). Whilst important efforts are being made to understand the social and cultural contexts of the families that they work with (Chapters 4, 10), it can be a challenge for practitioners to truly understand the diversity and the individual needs of children and parents. For instance, it may not always be easy to understand the different styles of parenting, methods of disciplining, and priorities for children's education that are held by parents from diverse communities. It is important that this should be considered if all parents are to feel that they can, and would like to, be involved in their children's learning.

For adults working with children, it is also important to recognize the continuity between home and school. As Hedegaard (2009: 72) emphasizes, 'children's development can be seen as socio-cultural tracks through different institutions'. In other words, children may be confronted with conflicting practices at home and at school if their homes have traditions and values that are different from those of the settings they attend. When there is a dissociation between home and school cultures, children can be disadvantaged, as their learning experience may be reinforced differently at home and at school (Shields, 2009). This disadvantage can be seen even more clearly in comparison with their peers who do not experience this dissociation. Those children whose parents have had positive experiences of schools in their childhood often have an understanding of the ways that early childhood settings work. They interact with their children in similar ways to those that are practised in these settings, enabling their children to feel at ease when they begin nursery. For other children, on the other hand, it could be a completely alien experience.

Furthermore, our understanding of the diversity of parents should be based on evidence, if we are to 'avoid categorizing, stereotyping, and impeding families through the work we develop with them' (Swick and Williams, 2006: 371). In some cases, practitioners may find it difficult to take the diversity of parents' needs, values and expectations into account, and to adjust their practice accordingly (Brooker, 2002; Crozier, 1999; Vincent, 1996). Parents' own experiences of schooling and of their teachers will have an influence on the way they perceive their children's learning. Parents who had a tough time at school themselves may find it difficult to relate to practitioners: they may find it particularly hard to enter the setting, let alone to have a meaningful conversation with members of staff. In addition, parents from 'poor or minority communities' (Brooker, 2002) are often expected to become involved in the same way as middle-class parents, but their backgrounds and past experiences may make them feel unable to do so. They may demonstrate their awareness that they do not know what is required of them and so can become more and more isolated from the other parents and from practitioners.

Working with parents from diverse communities

The parents who took part in the FRF project provide a good illustration of the diversity of parents in settings. I visited four families to show them a DVD recording of episodes of their children's creative thinking in the nursery. All were white working-class families who lived on the same estate in similar housing. Their children were similar ages and they attended the same Children's Centre. Initially, they also appeared to have similar back-grounds. Yet my home visit to them revealed that their beliefs and ways of parenting were very different. For instance, there was diversity in the ways in which the fathers got involved in their children's activities. They were all unemployed and were at home with their partners when I visited, so I was able to show the recording of their children to both parents. Two of the fathers proudly watched the DVD clips of their children with their partners. One exclaimed 'That's my boy!' as he watched his son playing on the keyboard. He asked detailed questions about his son's activities at nurs-ery. On the other hand, the fathers of the other two children left the room shortly after I arrived, leaving their partners to speak to me: 'He leaves me to deal with the kids' was one mother's explanation.

Whilst these four families appeared to be similar in many ways, the short visit to their homes made their diversity more obvious with respect to the fathers' involvement. A study by Hauari and Hollingworth (2009) illus-trates that the roles of the fathers have changed for some families, so that the mothers are no longer relied upon to take sole care of the children, even though the gender stereotype of mothers as the main carers still exists for them. Children whose fathers are present and who regularly join in in their activities will have different experiences from those whose fathers take on only a small part in their upbringing. This is not to suggest that some fathers in the FRF project were indifferent to children's experiences. Rather, it demonstrates the different ways in which partners express their involvement in children's activities.

Children from ethnic minority communities are also a diverse group, although the diversity of their needs is not always appreciated in early childhood practice. Parke and Drury (2000) suggest that parenting in these communities was often seen as deviating from the 'mainstream' parenting style by practitioners, rather than acknowledging it as a reflection of their cultural practice. Lahman and Park (2004) also point out that the mis-match between parents and practitioners in terms of their views of parenting 'may be even more extreme when families and teachers are from diverse cultures' (2004: 133). As we see in Chapter 10, whilst huge improvements are apparent in terms of practitioners understanding the social and cultural diversity of children and families, working with those from very different backgrounds from their own can still be a challenge.

For instance, one mother in the FRF project voiced her concern about how her parenting style and the value of education may be misunderstood by her son's teacher. She had just returned from a summer holiday in Kabul, Afghanistan, where she had been visiting relatives with her two children. Her daughter had remained mainly indoors with her when they were away whilst her son Koshan (not his real name) had spent all summer playing outside with other boys. When they returned to England, Koshan began primary school. His mother was very disappointed as the teachers had told her that he 'would not sit still and listen'. She had not discussed his experience during the summer with his teacher: '*[the teacher] did not ask and my English is not very good.*' She explained to me that when she was growing up in Afghanistan, she was not able to attend any form of education once she was 16 as by the time she reached that age, it had become impossible for women to go to schools. She saw education as something that is very precious, and was therefore upset by her conversation with the teacher who appeared to think that she did not value her son's time at school. It is not difficult to surmise that the teacher in this situation was also disappointed in her communication with Koshan's mother.

Another example comes from an African mother. She travels two hours each way by bus to take her son, Jared, to nursery because 'it's the only place I could find that would give him a free place and I want to be a nurse so I'm going to college'. She had nothing but praise for the nursery and was confident that he had learned a great deal since he had been attending. However, the transcript of a practitioner's discussion about Jared shows that she and possibly other members of staff already seem to have developed a deficit view of him and his capabilities. The discussion with his mother has not taken place at this stage. The practitioner suggests that he seems unable to answer questions put to him, perhaps reflecting lack of confidence in his ability to reply. The situation appears to reflect Souto-Manning and Swick's (2006: 188) suggestion that: 'Teachers may start out less than enthusiastic about parent partnerships and then have this reticence reinforced by bad situations or those about which they lack understanding'. In this way parents may inadvertently be discouraged from becoming full partners in their children's learning. Assumptions by both practitioners and parents about each other can create barriers even before they have begun to try to establish a relationship.

In one-to-one discussions at home, all of these parents demonstrated to me that they had a wealth of knowledge and insight about their own children. They spoke confidently about their children's abilities, but said that they had not shared much of this with their teachers. They had communicated some of the information to them but had 'held back' from providing a complete picture. This was partly because of the limited time they spent with teachers, and also because of the limited availability of the staff at the setting. One parent explained that since the setting had moved to a new building, there seemed to be more of a 'lock down' situation: practitioners seemed to be 'locked in' with the children. The family workers, however, were 'always around'. There could be many reasons for this and there is no doubt that practitioners had also attempted to communicate with the parents. These parents' experiences also raise further issues about the importance of making time and opportunities for them to get to know the practitioners, and vice versa.

Working with changing families

The involvement of parents in research and in early childhood practice is further complicated by the changing family unit in many of the industrialized countries. Stereotypical views about families may still be present in society and in the minds of some practitioners. Yet, societal views about marriage have changed drastically in recent years, and family structure is no longer solely comprised of married parents living with their children. Families are now a mix of cohabiting parents, stepfamilies, single parent families, those living apart or living together and civil partnerships, as well as the traditional nuclear family (Family Policy Social Centre, 2009). Life is therefore much more complicated for many families, and particularly for children who may spend part of the week with one parent in one family and another part of the week with the other parent in another family. This sometimes makes it difficult for practitioners to know which parents they should refer to, as some children may be involved in as many as five different families. In such cases, children may have to experience different parenting styles, which can be very confusing and leave them wondering which rules to follow. For researchers, asking which 'families' to take part in a project could therefore be a complex matter that requires close collaboration with practitioners.

 Case study

Jane brings her daughter Amy to nursery every day. She rarely speaks to anyone and always hurries away. The nursery staff have tried to involve her by asking her to help in various activities in the setting but she is never available. One day, Brenda, who is Amy's keyperson, arranges to visit them at home and takes some photographs of Amy playing at nursery. Jane is delighted and from then on she gradually begins to talk to staff when she collects Amy. She has explained to Brenda that her mum is disabled and so she cannot leave her on her own for long. She wants Amy to have the experience of her mother taking part in various activities in the setting, but is also worried about volunteering as she does not feel confident in helping at the nursery.

- Could something have been done sooner to involve Jane and Amy in the setting?

- What ways have been used in your setting to involve parents who seem reluctant?

- Have you ever made any assumptions about parents that you have later found to be untrue?

- What do you think changed Jane's mind and helped her to feel included?

- Is there anything you could do in your setting to help all parents feel included?

Parents' expectations of their children's learning

Peters et al. (2007) and Siraj-Blatchford's (2010b) studies draw attention to 'disadvantaged' parents and their involvement in their children's learning. Their studies make it clear that many of these parents need no persuasion to provide a good and supportive home learning environment for children. As Siraj-Blatchford (2010b: 463) suggests, disadvantaged families 'often have high aspirations for their children and provide significant educational support'. Some of the parents in the FRF study could also be said to be 'disadvantaged', yet they all valued their children's learning, citing, for example, the importance of providing opportunities to enjoy writing, reading books and counting. These parents also acknowledged the importance of children's play and imagination. One couple particularly encouraged role play at home. Their son often played with 'small world people' in the bath and could be heard saying phrases such as: 'I'll rescue you, help! I'm drowning!' These parents mentioned that their son would become 'either a footballer or a doctor'.

Another parent spoke about her anxiety that her daughter had not achieved as much as she needed to before starting school: 'I need to get her up to speed with writing before she starts school'. This possibly suggests a discrepancy between the expectations of children's learning by practitioners and parents. It could also indicate that the setting has not communicated its aims and objectives for the children to the parents in the ways parents can understand. It is also possible that the parents told me more about their aspirations for their children than they had told the practitioners. They may have found it easier to talk to me as a researcher, sitting in their living rooms listening and not providing any advice, especially as confidentiality was assured.

Challenges in involving parents in research

Involving parents in research should enable the researchers to listen to their voices and to scrutinize different understandings of the ways in which they involve themselves in children's learning. As suggested earlier, involving parents in research may sound easy, but many difficulties arise in between planning the research and disseminating its findings. For instance, Crozier (2003) highlights the problems of disseminating any research that includes parents' voices:

> ... you parade someone else's lifestyle and identity in front of an audience, thus laying it open to judgement. Should the researcher 'tell it how it is'? Is that what is meant by 'giving a voice'? Or should the researcher present what she sees/hears in a way that she thinks will protect the respondent or be acceptable (or is that palatable?) to the audience? (2003: 79)

All parents want the best for their children, but some things 'get in the way' of providing children with home environments that are conducive to their learning. Is it right that research should highlight the problems that exist, so that parents are made more aware of any shortcomings they may have?

In the FRF project, parents allowed me to enter their homes and spoke to me openly about their children and their lives. They gave me clear insights into their aims and objectives for their children, but also spoke of more intimate details. They demonstrated a trust that I would be a considerate custodian of the information. The ways in which the data is analysed must not betray that trust. For instance, there are some details that may be left out of the analysis to maintain the anonymity of the participants. Which part of the data to omit and which to include requires sensitivity on the part of researchers: our understanding of the social and cultural contexts of the parents should help us to make these decisions.

All those interviewed in the FRF project were volunteers, seemed happy to give up their time, and made me welcome in their homes: yet there were many who did not wish to take part. They could be those frequently described in the literature as 'hard to reach' parents, whose participation would have provided further insight into the issue of parental involvement. My own time constraints also prevented me from interviewing all those parents who were willing to take part, which raises the issue of excluding some parents' voices from research. However, whilst acknowledging that the sample of parents whom I interviewed in the FRF project was relatively small, and by no means representative of parents in England, they nevertheless gave me a deeper understanding of the dilemmas many parents face in getting involved in their children's learning.

Conclusion

The involvement of all parents in their children's learning is never going to be easy. Now that communities are becoming more diverse, practitioners have to 'bridge the perspectives of parents and themselves' (Lahman and Park, 2004). They need to gain an understanding of many different cultures and practices alongside all the other responsibilities they have, and then to form relationships with parents that demonstrate trust and consideration. In some cases, parents may be heavily involved in children's learning without appearing to be so, as they may fail to communicate their involvement to practitioners, as the discussion above suggests.

What is certain is that most parents know what they want for their children. It is vital that practitioners discover this so that they can work with parents in order to gain mutual understanding of their children's learning, and provide support both in the setting and at home. Other interventions (such as parenting classes) may be necessary to build on this understanding, but first, the trust and respect between practitioner and parent needs to be fostered.

One of the implications for involving parents in research is that researchers must appreciate the great diversity of parents and changing families, and this involves critical reflection upon the way in which we conduct ourselves in research. Researchers need to form a collaborative relationship with practitioners (Chapter 7) and to build on their experience of involving parents in early childhood settings. The involvement of parents in the FRF project demonstrates the anxiety that many of them experience as they enter early childhood settings. We need to listen carefully to their views so as to contribute to the enhancement of the quality of early childhood practice.

Reflection

If you are a practitioner, think of the parents you work with:

- Do you speak to some more often than others? If so why is this?
- Are there some parents you rarely speak to? What could you do to change this?
- If you were conducting research with parents, how would you approach them, and what would you do to build a trusting relationship with them?

Researchers and practitioners collaborating on research

Hiroko Fumoto

This chapter focuses on:

- The tension between qualitative and quantitative approaches in early childhood research;

- Three main ideas in a mixed methods approach: 'abductive reasoning'; intersubjectivity, and the view of quantitative research as an interpretive activity;

- The implications of these ideas for thinking about researchers and practitioners collaborating on research.

Collaboration between researchers and practitioners has been seen as a critical part of research in early childhood settings, and this is partly based on two significant developments. The first is the growing importance placed upon democratizing the process of conducting research (Anning, 2010). Just as the early childhood community has come to see children's development from various socio-cultural perspectives (Fleer and Robbins, 2007), so it has begun to embrace the notion of research as a way of collaboratively constructing knowledge. Practitioners are no longer seen simply as a source of data, or as gatekeepers to researchers' access to settings, and to children and their families. Instead, these relationships are increasingly seen as 'collaborative'.

The second development is in the importance placed upon knowledge that is produced through practice (Edwards et al., 2007). This arises from concerns about the ways in which research has had limited impact on practice, despite the positive intentions of many projects in this respect (Edwards et al., 2007). In collaborative research, practitioners play a significant role in identifying issues that need to be investigated, and in offering their interpretations in data analysis. Research with practitioners can also 'generate change in practice' from within (Edwards, 2007). Thus, their involvement in the process of research has become vital in enhancing the relevance of research to practice and in adding credibility to research activities.

The question here is: what are the implications of the notion of collaboration for the ways in which we do research? The idea of 'co-constructing' knowledge with practitioners (or with other research participants) reflects interpretivism, or social constructivism, often associated with qualitative methods. Does this mean that quantitative research, which is generally associated with positivism/post-positivism, cannot be collaborative in the sense that it does not offer practitioners the same level of involvement as does qualitative research? This chapter considers the mixed methods approaches to research, that is, integrating qualitative and quantitative methods, as a way to address this issue.

Tensions in early childhood research

Some of the tension in the field appears to involve the ways in which researchers make use of qualitative and quantitative methods in their investigations. For instance, many researchers have embraced qualitative research as the best way to explore the complexities of children's lives. This movement may have led them away from quantitative research and towards a firm rejection of a 'normalized' view of children's development that has often (perhaps wrongly) been associated with developmental psychology: some research in this field has been criticized for not paying enough attention to the complexities of participants' lives, their backgrounds, their thoughts and emotions (e.g. New, 2008).

Where collaborative research is concerned, qualitative approaches typically involve listening to children, families and practitioners, such that the diversity of their views and experiences can be investigated. In relation to this, Pascal and Bertram (2009) talk about a 'participatory paradigm' in which research and practice are based on valuing 'the diversity of cultures and world views' (2009: 257). This also reflects socio-constructivist or interpretative paradigms, in which the social process of constructing knowledge is seen as significant. As Creswell and Plano Clark (2011) note, a qualitative approach is accepted by researchers who take a 'collaborative stance', as it provides ways of involving participants in various aspects of the investigation. On the other hand, the notion of collaboration may not appear to fit so well with the quantitative approach to research. This approach is generally seen as being conducted by researchers in order to test their hypotheses, rather than being based on shared objectives negotiated with participants. Its general aim is often to understand the overall patterns of phenomena by identifying the associations between variables (e.g. between teachers' perceptions of teacher–child relationships and children's well-being).

Part of the reason for the tension may lie in the backgrounds of researchers. For instance, there may be more researchers in the early childhood field who have had first-hand experience in settings, not only as researchers but also as practitioners, in comparison with their counterparts in psychological research. First-hand experiences imply a degree of emotional investment in the field, which underpins the construction of an epistemological standpoint of the world (Merleau-Ponty, 1962). Researchers with first-hand experience in the field may be more likely to suggest that a positivistic approach is not suitable for investigating the 'multiple realities' of phenomena that concern children: they may be more inclined to focus on individual cases because of their experience of having emotionally invested in individual children in a particular setting. Our experiences can serve as a powerful motivator in deciding the kind of research that we do.

The tensions between researchers working in different methodological traditions and between the use of qualitative and quantitative approaches, is problematic, especially when there is a lack of communication between the two. Opportunities to make use of the best of both approaches may be missed, along with the development of multiple ways of addressing issues that matter to practitioners, and to children and their families.

The mixed methods approach: crossing the boundaries between qualitative and quantitative approaches

According to Tashakkori and Creswell (2007: 4), mixed methods research can be defined as: '... research in which the investigator collects and analyzes data, integrates the findings, and draws inferences using both qualitative and quantitative approaches or methods in a single study or a program of inquiry'. Different authors describe this approach in diverse ways, however. For instance, there are those who describe the mixed methods approach as the combination of different qualitative or quantitative methods within a project (e.g. Alexander et al., 2008). Others have used different terminologies such as 'combining' and 'integrating' methods (e.g. Bryman, 2007). In this chapter, we will refer to mixed methods approaches to research as those involving qualitative and quantitative approaches, and that attempt to make sense of phenomena by making use of findings from both approaches (e.g. Creswell and Plano Clark, 2011).

Whilst a number of authors have employed mixed methods approaches in their investigations (e.g. Levin-Rozalis, 2004; Nichols, et al., 2009; Siraj-Blatchford and Manni, 2008), their use has been fraught with controversy. For instance, there is a long-standing debate about the differences between qualitative and quantitative approaches in terms of their ontological, epistemological and methodological underpinnings. The differences between qualitative and quantitative approaches are seen as insurmountable by some, particularly as they are based on a fundamental disagreement about 'what could be known' (D.L. Morgan, 2007: 58). According to D.L. Morgan (2007), the difficulty stems partly from the ways in which the tension between qualitative and quantitative approaches is about more than just the methods that researchers employ in their investigations, and has come to involve researchers' 'belief systems', and their 'ontological assumptions about the nature of reality and truth' (2007: 57).

In D.L. Morgan's view, part of the problem lies in the ways in which the term 'research paradigm' has evolved. This is often conceptualized as researchers' 'world views', that is, the ways in which we see the world. He argues that this way of considering different research paradigms is too broad as it 'includes virtually *everything* someone thinks or believes' (2007: 52), and suggests the need to clarify what constitutes our world views. For him, one aspect of these views is the 'shared beliefs within a community of researchers who share a consensus about which questions are most meaningful and which procedures are most appropriate for answering those questions' (2007: 53). This way of thinking about research paradigms reveals how 'human agency' plays a part in constructing the boundaries between research paradigms (D.L. Morgan, 2007).

Over the years, 'pragmatism' has emerged as an alternative research paradigm that is associated with mixed methods research (e.g. Creswell, 2009; Johnson and Onwuegbuzie, 2004). Central to this approach is the 'meaningful communication between researchers who pursue different approaches to their field' (D.L. Morgan, 2007: 67). Three concepts are particularly relevant in breaking down the barriers between qualitative and quantitative approaches further, and in considering the issue of collaboration between researchers and practitioners, and are addressed in the next three sections.

'Abductive reasoning'

This refers to the ways in which researchers move back and forth between induction and deduction in their efforts to explore social phenomena (D.L. Morgan, 2007). Whilst the notions of induction and deduction are often seen as separate processes that are associated with qualitative and quantitative approaches respectively, the distinction is less clear-cut in the real world:

Try to imagine acting in the real world for as long as 5 minutes while operating in

either a strictly theory-driven deductive mode or a data-driven, inductive mode –
I certainly would not want to be on the same road as anyone who had such a
fatally limited approach to driving a vehicle! (D.L. Morgan, 2007: 71)

Abductive reasoning enables us to conceptualize how we can apply both
inductive and deductive reasoning when we try and make sense of social
phenomena, rather than adhering to one way of reasoning.

In the FRF project, we have employed both inductive and deductive reasoning to examine the ways in which practitioners promote children's
creative thinking. For example, we used a qualitative interview study in
our first phase to explore practitioners' views about children's creative
thinking (Robson and Hargreaves, 2005). Building on this, we conducted a
quantitative questionnaire survey to examine practitioners' experiences of
the time available to facilitate children's thinking. This phase also
employed a qualitative approach to elicit individual practitioners' experiences of this (Fumoto and Robson, 2006). We then further explored the
practitioners' experiences of supporting children's thinking with particular
reference to the personal ownership and autonomy felt in their practice
(Robson and Fumoto, 2009). This moving back and forth between inductive and deductive approaches to research has been helpful in forming a
deep and broad understanding of the topic.

In addition, according to D.L. Morgan (2007), abductive reasoning allows
us to move back and forth between studies that employ quantitative or
qualitative approaches, rather than dismissing others' studies as 'based on
wholly incompatible assumptions' (2007: 71). This is important as it allows
us to consult a wide range of literature when we justify our research question. It also enables us to put our investigation into perspective when we
are conducting either qualitative or quantitative research.

Intersubjectivity

According to D.L. Morgan (2007), intersubjectivity plays a key role in a
mixed methods approach. Research, in his view, is fundamentally a social
process in which researchers and participants come to develop some kind
of shared meaning about the aims and objectives of research, and the
methods that are employed for investigation. This also relates to the
notion of 'the communities of practice approach to research paradigms',
whereby researchers working in qualitative or quantitative research traditions, and the participants of that research, come together to explore social
phenomena or issues that concern them (Denscombe, 2008: 278). Here,
Denscombe explains that 'membership' of communities of practice is
'open to change' (2008: 278), implying that the boundaries of research
paradigms are fluid. Deriving from Lave and Wenger's (1991) work, this
emphasizes the social process of knowledge construction. Learning, seen in

this way, is 'a collective activity' (Denscombe, 2008: 276): and in the case of research in early childhood settings, it is a collective activity between researchers and practitioners, and indeed between children and families.

For D.L. Morgan (2007), the goal of a mixed methods approach is to 'search for useful points of connection' between qualitative and quantitative approaches (2007: 71). In discussing this, he once again rejects the dichotomy between qualitative and quantitative approaches. For instance, he rejects the clear-cut division between subjectivity and objectivity that is often associated with qualitative and quantitative approaches respectively, acknowledging the impossibility (and undesirability) of either complete objectivity or subjectivity in research. He also rejects the distinctions between 'specific and context-dependent' (qualitative approach) or 'universal and generalized' (quantitative approach) that arise in debating the usefulness of these approaches, emphasizing the importance of working back and forth between 'specific results and their more general implications' in order to gain a fuller picture of the phenomena under investigation (2007: 72).

In order to search for 'connections' between qualitative and quantitative approaches, Westerman (2006) also emphasizes the importance of open communication between researchers employing diverse research methods. Greene (2008) further echoes this view and talks about 'a mixed methods way of thinking' as:

> ... an orientation towards social inquiry that actively invites us to participate in dialogue about multiple ways of seeing and hearing, multiple ways of making sense of the social world, and multiple standpoints on what is important and to be valued and cherished. (Greene, 2008: 20)

In essence, the importance lies in 'respectful listening and understanding' between researchers (Greene, 2008: 20).

Quantitative research as interpretative activity

Westerman (2006) suggests that the use of quantitative approaches in social research involves a great deal of interpretation by researchers and often by participants, and that its association with positivism is a misconception. According to Westerman, the social world is not out there to be measured. Rather, when we are trying to understand a phenomenon, we are not 'outsiders looking into' it in a dispassionate fashion, but are already a part of what we are about to investigate.

In the case of measurement that uses Likert-type scales, for instance, each item (i.e. a question) is constructed on the basis of 'rich appreciation of the meanings of human behavior' (Westerman, 2006: 191), and the ways in which participants respond to each question are not mechanical. Participants also bring their own interpretations to the questions that they are answering, and therefore, when researchers analyse the data, an element of social construction is occurring between the researchers and the participants. Westerman points out that measurement in quantitative research is often mistakenly considered to be a more objective way of understanding phenomena than using a qualitative approach: but the process of constructing a measurement is based on the decisions we make. Statistical analysis may be used in this process, yet this also involves interpretation, because the decisions as to which statistical procedures to use, and how to interpret the results, all rest on the researchers' interpretation of the issue under investigation (Westerman, 2006). As Westerman emphasizes: '... the key point here is that even though mathematics enters into the picture via data analysis, our examination of phenomena is *not* mathematical in nature' (2006: 194).

Mixed methods research and collaborating with practitioners

So far, we have considered the issues concerning the mixed methods approach, and how it may be useful in crossing the boundaries between qualitative and quantitative approaches. There are several implications for research with practitioners.

Practitioners as part of research communities

As referred to earlier, the idea of the 'communities of practice' approach to research (Denscombe, 2008) plays an important part in mixed methods research. This approach facilitates the ways in which researchers from diverse backgrounds, who have been trained in the use of different methods, can come together to investigate a particular social phenomenon, adding richness to their work. For instance, as mentioned at the outset of this book, the researchers in the FRF project come from diverse professional and academic backgrounds and have different research interests. Whilst these differences bring challenges, as we may not always agree on everything, the diversity provides us with various ways of exploring young children's creative thinking and the ways in which parents and practitioners promote this. It also presents an opportunity to question our own assumptions about research and about issues concerning children's creative thinking. There is always a limit to what one researcher can do, but as 'communities of practice', we can broaden our investigations.

The idea of communities of practice also provides grounds for involving research participants as part of these communities. In the case of research conducted in early childhood settings the practitioners, as professionals working directly with young children, play an important role in this process. The key to collaboration between practitioners and researchers is the researchers' openness to communicating with practitioners about the research, and to listening to their experiences in this process: this represents what we referred to earlier as 'pragmatism'. Furthermore, the emphasis on intersubjectivity in the mixed methods approach (e.g. D.L. Morgan, 2007) highlights the importance of the interpersonal relationships that develop between practitioners and researchers. When we look back at our work with practitioners in research projects, we may feel that we may not have always been successful in putting these principles into practice, even though our intention to do so was genuine: I will return to this point later.

Continuous reflection on the ways we do research and readiness to make adjustment. To develop relationships that make collaboration possible requires time, and the researchers' ability to see the process of research from practitioners' perspectives. Some of the questions that need to be asked at the planning stage of research may be: Would I want to be a participant in this particular project that I am proposing? Would I be comfortable in replying to these questions posed in interviews or in questionnaires? Would I feel comfortable to be observed by a researcher when I am interacting with children? If the answers to these questions are 'no', or even 'unsure', then we need to readjust the ways in which the research is conducted. Indeed, practitioners are busy people, and the importance of seeing the process of research from their points of view cannot be overstated (see the case study in this chapter).

Collaboration in any task is not an easy process. Collaborators have different agendas, time scales, and personalities, all of which affect the ways we interact with others. We often talk about 'shared understanding', but this may not always be constant. We need to continuously negotiate the meanings we attach to issues under investigation.

Making decisions and the ways in which practitioners are positioned in the process of research. In doing research, many decisions are made not only about what we want to investigate and how we go about doing this, but also about the ways in which practitioners are positioned in the process. As the foregoing discussion suggests, collaboration with practitioners can work in different ways and at different levels of intensity, depending on the ways in which the study is designed. This, in turn, is influenced by the myriad of decisions that we make in the process.

For instance, when exploring teacher–child relationships in early childhood settings in a study related to the FRF project, we decided that our focus would be on teachers' perceptions of their relationships with children, rather than on children's and parents' experiences of relating to their teachers (Fumoto et al., 2003, 2007). The assumption was that teachers are professionals who are committed to improving their practice, and we wanted to leave it to them to reflect on children's and parents' experiences when it came to something as sensitive as teacher–child relationships. The role of research, in this case, was to facilitate their reflection.

Furthermore, asking children and parents about their relationships with their teachers could also raise ethical issues. The mere fact that a researcher starts asking them about their teachers might make them think about the issue in ways that may, in turn, inadvertently affect these relationships. In hindsight, our investigation of parents and children's experiences of relating their teachers may have been an important avenue of research that might have further developed our understanding about the complexities of teacher–child relationships. It might have also helped teachers in their reflection. However, the decisions we made were based on the ways in which we position teachers in our investigation at the time, and this certainly provides us with a great deal to reflect upon.

Numerical data and practitioners' voices

The earlier discussion emphasizes the importance of the ways in which we associate numerical data with the participants' voices. Rather than seeing the data as something that is completely 'objective', we have suggested the importance of considering the roles that 'interpretation' and 'meaning' play in quantitative research. To take teacher–child relationships research as an example, the Student–Teacher Relationship Scale (STRS) is a 28-item scale, based on a Likert-type format, designed to assess practitioners' perceptions of their relationships with a particular child (Pianta, 2001). It contains statements such as 'I share an affectionate, warm relationship with this child' and 'Despite my best efforts, I'm uncomfortable with how this child and I get along'. Practitioners provide a great deal of interpretation in the process of completing this scale. For instance, one of the practitioners who completed the STRS for her group of children noted:

> ... there's a specific question that says, something like, 'do children perceive you as being negative towards them' or something. And I've put definitely no (laugh) on everyone. Because that is what my hope is. I'm hoping that they don't. Then I'm thinking, oh was that child OK, because I know that I always say, don't do that or remember this, and you know, do children see me as this authoritarian person who's completely in control? And I think probably they do more than I want to admit to myself, so I mean, that kind of makes you think about your practice. (Fumoto, 2005)

Employing measurement instruments such as STRS along with qualitative interviews makes us aware that practitioners' thoughts and reflections underlie numerical data. Mixed methods research provides us with the opportunity to make further connections between quantitative and qualitative data in order to make sense of practitioners' experiences.

Ethical considerations

Ethics not only involve the ways in which we pay attention to technical aspects of our research, such as ensuring confidentiality and the anonymity of the participants, but also involve our sensitivity to the ways in which participants experience the process of research. Our ethical considerations should apply from the time we formulate our research questions right through to the time we report the findings. We may design a study that involves collaboration, but if we do not develop relationships with participants that are based on trust and respect the investigation becomes futile, regardless of the methods that we employ.

Gorard and Taylor (2004) remind us of the importance of maintaining the 'quality and rigour' of research as part of the researchers' 'ethical responsibility' (2004: 172). They suggest that this issue has not attracted enough attention when it comes to considering ethics in research, and emphasize the importance of using an appropriate method of investigation as part of this process. That is, if a mixed methods approach provides a better way of investigating the phenomena in question than either qualitative or quantitative methods alone, then it should be used so as to ensure that the research will reach a useful conclusion. The same can be said about choosing qualitative or quantitative methods in our inquiries. As Gorard and Taylor put it: 'Pointless research ... remains pointless however "ethically" it appears to be conducted. Good intentions do not guarantee good outcomes' (2004: 173). Whilst what counts as a 'good outcome' is debatable, this nevertheless reminds us that upholding the quality of research should be our priority. For research in early childhood settings, this involves our deep reflection about the ways in which researchers work with practitioners.

 Case study

> Sheila is a teacher who works in a private preschool programme in the USA. She works with an assistant teacher and with a group of 3-year-olds, and her work experience with young children extends to 29 years. She took part in a research project that involves once-a-week participant observations throughout a school year. During the interview, she commented:
>
> > I wasn't necessarily looking forward to [being observed] at first because I didn't know what to expect. But I got to the stage where it didn't bother me at all. You [the researcher] were like a third teacher ... [I would recommend the experience to other teachers] because I felt good about it. I think most people do not like to be observed because they feel threatened. I don't think that's unusual ... but I'd do it again!
>
> How would you feel if you were asked to be observed for a whole school year? What should researchers do to ease the initial anxiety?

Conclusion

In early childhood research, the researchers often intend to collaborate with practitioners. However, this 'intention' requires critical reflection: how does the process of research look from practitioners' points of view? Do they feel that it is based on collaboration with the researcher: and do they feel that they are respected, trusted and that their views are being listened to?

We are not by any means advocating that all researchers should employ mixed methods approaches in their investigations; but we have emphasized the importance of developing meaningful communication between researchers based in different methodological traditions. This could be through further developing the 'communities of practice approach' to research, and through making use of a wide range of literature that is based on diverse approaches to research, without dismissing those that may not meet our own preferred approach. In the case of research conducted in early childhood settings, practitioners are critical members of the communities, sharing with researchers a commitment to enhancing the quality of early childhood practice. The intersubjectivity of mixed methods approaches provides a useful perspective on social relationships by placing these at their heart.

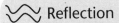 Reflection

- Develop a list of things that you would need to consider in conducting collaborative research with practitioners. Discuss how you are going to achieve them.
- Think about extending your research project by applying a mixed methods approach. If you are already employing this approach, provide a rationale for doing so.
- Consider the 'communities of practice' approach to research. Who are the members of your research communities? Who is included and why? Who is missing and why?

Part 3

Experiences of Young Children, Parents and Practitioners

The third part of the book has three chapters which are based on our findings in the FRF research: these are documented in full in various journal articles, and so this part of the book represents a broad overview of the project. We deal with these findings from the points of view of the children (Chapter 8), the parents (Chapter 9), and the practitioners (Chapter 10) respectively. Whilst this enables us to make sense of a large body of data in a reasonably clear and straightforward fashion, it is important to bear in mind that each one of these three perspectives is intricately bound up with both of the other two. Parents' views of their children's learning, for example, are powerfully influenced not only by what their children tell them about their experiences in the setting, but also by their perceptions of the practitioners' views of themselves and of their children: in this sense, all of these different points of view are interdependent.

In Chapter 8, Sue Robson emphasizes the value of observing children's everyday activities in providing evidence of their creative thinking, and describes the development of the *Analysing Children's Creative Thinking* (ACCT) Framework in our research. This is a research and practice tool which we have used for identifying and supporting young children's creative thinking. It is based on three main aspects of their behaviour, namely *exploration*, *involvement* and *persistence*, each of which we consider to be an indicator of children's creative thinking, and each of which she considers in turn. She also looks at the role of children's choice and ownership of different activities in their creative thinking, and considers the social contexts and activities that support this.

In Chapter 9, Sue Greenfield focuses on the parents' perspectives: this part of our research clearly shows that parents' views of their relationships with practitioners are often not only inaccurate, but can also show basic mis-understandings of their mutual roles. Because of this, she is able to demonstrate the value of using video-recorded episodes during home vis-its to parents. Parents often show great surprise when viewing recordings of their children in the settings because they behave in ways which are very different from their typical behaviour at home. She also looks in more detail at parents' interpretations of the connections between what children do at home and in the early childhood setting, and at their views of the relationships between their children's behaviour at home, and their under-standing of creative thinking.

In Chapter 10, Hiroko Fumoto considers the challenges that practitioners face in promoting children's creative thinking: these include the limited time which is available to spend with children given all the other demands placed upon them, such as record-keeping and other paperwork; trying to meet the needs of individual children when they are working in groups; issues which arise from social and cultural diversity amongst the children; and the gap between theory and practice. She goes on to examine the likely effects of the different attributes which practitioners bring to their practice, including their professional autonomy; their ability to display 'flow' in their teamwork with other practitioners and with the children; and their professional commitment to getting to know individual children and their parents. All of these factors have important implications for pol-icy, professional development and research.

Children's experiences of creative thinking

Sue Robson

This chapter focuses on:

- The value of observing children's everyday activities for evidence of their creative thinking;

- The development of the *Analysing Children's Creative Thinking* (ACCT) Framework, a research and practice tool, for identifying and supporting young children's creative thinking;

- Children's exploration, involvement and persistence as indicators of their creative thinking;

- Children's choice and ownership and their creative thinking;

- Social contexts and activities that support children's creative thinking.

Developing an approach to identifying and analysing creative thinking in young children

Identifying thinking is always challenging, whether it is in adults, or in young children. In this chapter, we look at the evidence of young children's creative thinking collected during the FRF project. Our analysis of current theory and research on creative thinking, and of existing approaches to identifying it (see Chapters 2 and 3), led us to take account of both the conditions under which young children might most characteristically display their creative thinking, and of the indicative behaviour to look for.

The most common approaches to identifying creative thinking have tended to be psychometric tests (Burnard et al., 2008), particularly the Torrance Tests of Creative Thinking (TTCT), which are designed for children from Kindergarten onwards, and are used in more research than any other creativity test (Kim et al., 2006). These tests often emphasize divergent thinking. This may be helpful in identifying originality, but it nevertheless represents only a part of creative thinking, and not the whole picture.

For young children in particular, there may be two very fundamental ways in which tests such as the TTCT are less valuable or even misleading. First, young children may not have the best chance of displaying their true understanding in test situations because of communicative rather than cognitive difficulties (Samuelsson and Pramling, 2009). Second, the Torrance tests focus on participants' performances in disembedded situations, which may not give young children the best opportunities to display their competence or understanding. Donaldson's classic work (1978), subsequently corroborated by others, demonstrated that young children perform most effectively in contexts which make sense to them, and to which they can relate from experience. This suggested to us that focusing on young children as they engaged in meaningful, everyday activities could be more valuable in revealing the depth and breadth of their creative thinking than looking at them in test situations. This, in turn, showed the value of narrative observation. Observations cannot, of course, tell us directly what a child is thinking, but they can provide us with evidence of behaviour that may indicate aspects of his/her thinking. As Sylva et al. (1980: 10) suggest, 'young children do communicate much about their inner thoughts and emotions by overt behaviour'.

Alongside observations, the focus in this chapter is on the ways in which children talk *about* their thoughts and ideas. Vygotsky (1986) views language, and in particular dialogue, as a key psychological tool for children to both express and develop their thoughts. Pramling (1988) demonstrates the ways in which explicit talk about learning and thinking may help young children become more aware of their thinking, a finding also supported by the FRF project (Robson and Hargreaves, 2005). Reflective dialogues (RDs) with practitioners and researchers, therefore, should support children's own reflections about their actions and, in turn, give us valuable insights into their thoughts and ideas (Chapter 3).

A framework for observing and analysing young children's creative thinking

The research, theory and practice discussed in Chapters 2 and 3 are central to the development of the observation-led *Analysing Children's Creative Thinking* (ACCT) Framework (Table 8.1), which was developed in

Table 8.1 The *Analysing Children's Creative Thinking* Framework, with examples from the FRF project (children aged 3–5 years)

Category	Operational Definition	Example
E: EXPLORATION		
E1: Exploring	Child is keen to explore, and/or shows interest in the potential of a material or activity.	J is trying out buttons on the keyboard, causing a rhythm to play. He plays individual notes with alternate hands, smiling and watching carefully as he makes a note pattern.
E2: Engaging in new activity	Child is interested in becoming involved in an activity and taking an idea forward. The activity could be of his/her own choice or suggested by another child or adult.	A approaches a table covered in paint, where children previously have been working. She picks up a piece of paper from a pile and lays it on the table. Turning it over she spreads the paint that is now printed on it with her fingers.
E3: Knowing what you want to do	Child shows enjoyment or curiosity when choosing to engage in an activity.	K and adult A are standing at the woodwork bench. K has chosen a piece of wood, which he holds. He points to the back of the bench: 'In there'.
I: INVOLVEMENT & ENJOYMENT		
I1: Trying out	Child shows evidence of novel ways of looking and planning: uses prior knowledge or acquires new knowledge to imagine and/or hypothesize, or to show flexibility and originality in his/her thinking.	A is in the block area. She picks up three semi-circular blocks and lays two of them on the floor to form a circle, which she later calls a 'cheese'. She then puts one foot on each block and 'skates' across the carpet on them.
I2: Analysing ideas	Child shows either verbal or behavioural evidence of weighing up his/her idea, and deciding whether or not to pursue it.	R, N and K are building a tunnel from construction pieces. R watches as N and K build a cuboid, N puts a piece in front of the open end. R: 'No, they won't be able to get out.'
I3: Speculating	Child makes a speculative statement or asks a question of him/herself, or of other children or adults, relating to the activity.	H is outside, looking at herbs in the garden with adult J. H points to a herb and says 'Yes, but why is this spiky?'
I4: Involving others	Child engages with one or more children or adults to develop an idea or activity: may articulate an idea, seek to persuade others, or show receptivity to the ideas of others.	A, J and C are playing a 'Father Christmas' game in the block area. A: I'm Rudolph. J: And he's Rudolph too … No, he … you can be … C: (to A) You Comet, you be. A: (to C) Why don't you be Comet? C: No, I'm Donner.
P: PERSISTENCE		
P1: Persisting	Child shows resilience, and maintains involvement in an activity in the face of difficulty, challenge or uncertainty. He/she tolerates ambiguity.	In the sandpit E has been filling a large tube with dry sand. He picks up the tube and goes to fill the hopper on a nearby toy lorry, but the sand runs out of the end of the tube. He looks up, smiles, but does not break his concentration; instead he uses his hands to fill the hopper.
P2: Risk taking	Child displays a willingness to take risks, and to learn from mistakes.	M is at the clay. She tries to fill a bottle by inverting it into a full cup of water, but this causes the water to flow out on to the table. She abandons this and pours water straight from the cup onto the clay.
P3: Completing challenges	Child shows a sense of self-efficacy, self-belief and pleasure in achievement: shows conscious awareness of his/her own thinking.	M has been at the mark-making table, using felt tip pens and paper. He finishes his drawing. M: I've finished (smiling). Adult: Mm. M pats the paper and nods, then picks up the pen and makes a large 'M' in the bottom right corner. 'That's my Muh.' (He continues to write the other letters of his name.) 'I did it, I writ my name myself'.

collaboration with practitioners in the FRF project. The ACCT Framework incorporates social, emotional and cognitive dimensions, and consists of three categories: *Exploration, Involvement and Enjoyment*, and *Persistence*. The development of the ACCT Framework is an attempt to capture the richness and diversity of the actions, processes and behavioural dispositions that may contribute to creative thinking. In the ACCT Framework, the categories and their sub-components act as a series of potential indicators of creative thinking rather than as a checklist of qualifying conditions for creativity. The ACCT Framework does not require young children to display a particular number of these categories in order for their activities to count as evidence of 'creative thinking'. Rather, each piece of evidence helps to build a picture of a child's thinking.

The ACCT Framework has proved to be an effective research tool. However, just as importantly, it has also been useful for practitioners as it helps to highlight the occurrence of young children's creative thinking, and provides support for planning for their activities. The examples in Table 8.1 illustrate how seemingly simple, often quite slight, actions, gestures and comments from children may indicate creative thinking. All of this evidence comes together to provide a 'bigger picture', and thereby to support researchers and practitioners in 'spotting' children's creative thinking.

We now turn to what the evidence from the FRF project tells us about young children's creative thinking. We see the children as they engage in their everyday activities in settings, playing alone and with one another, and interacting with a range of adults, including teachers, nursery nurses, special educational needs (SEN) teachers, teaching assistants, and specialists such as visiting artists and musicians.

Most importantly, all children showed evidence of creative thinking according to the ACCT Framework, although this was more frequent in some than in others. The occurrence of examples of creative thinking (an action, gesture, or talk of some kind) varied from about every 11 seconds to every 72 seconds across all of the activities and over all of the children. This chapter is not the place to look at how these figures were obtained in detail, but it is helpful to note that, in the rest of the discussion, we refer to 'high' frequencies of examples of creative thinking as anything up to every 30 seconds, 'medium' as frequencies of between every 31 and 50 seconds, and 'low' frequency as less than every 50 seconds.

Some of the examples discussed in this chapter feature activities often seen as 'creative', such as music, dance, mark-making and representation in 2D and 3D media. However, along with these are examples of children displaying and developing creative thinking when engaged in pretence, mathematics and language activities, ICT, construction, sand and water, gardening and play of all kinds, both indoors and outside. Many of these are areas often not included in definitions of 'creative' activity. Significantly, for practitioners seeking to develop young children's creative thinking, the so-called 'creative' activities were no better at supporting and developing young children's creative thinking than any other type of activity. Overall, about half of the episodes in 'creative' activities led to the medium and higher frequencies of creative thinking. In the case of 'non-creative' activities, this figure rose to nearly three-quarters. Why should this be? The following sections offer some possible reasons, including the fact that 'creative' activities in our sample were often associated with adult direction, and were more likely to take place indoors. These two factors, as we shall see, seem to have an impact on young children's creative thinking.

Choice and ownership and young children's creative thinking

The balance between child- and adult-initiated activities in early childhood settings is a subject of much debate. Sylva et al. (2010) found that the 'excellent' and 'good' settings in their English study tended to have an equal balance between these activities. In the FRF project, those practitioners working with children aged 3 and 4 tended to place more emphasis on child-initiated activities, whilst those practitioners working with 4- and 5-year-olds were more likely to favour an equal division between child-initiated and adult-led activities.

It is useful to look at why this might be important, and what relationship it has to young children's creative thinking. As we saw in Chapter 3, the process of problem solving is clearly related to creative thinking. Tuma and Reif (1980) suggest that, when adults set a problem for children to solve, the children give fewer and less varied responses than when they identify and solve their own problems (Tuma and Reif, 1980, cited in de Boo 1999). In the FRF project, we found that the children's opportunities for choice, and the presence or absence of adult involvement in their activities, had a range of impacts on the ways in which they solved problems and demonstrated their creative thinking.

Choice and ownership

Exploration

In discussion in the RDs, children often talked about making their own choices to enter an activity, with the presence of friends frequently cited as a reason for becoming engaged. Interestingly, though, our observations of their activities suggest that adults had a significant impact on their initial engagement and exploration. The data show that, whilst children were least likely to become engaged in an activity when it was initiated and directed by an adult, they were more likely to show evidence of exploration and engagement in a new activity when an adult was present (but not directing the activity). On some occasions, adults actively engaged a child's interest when they saw what children were doing. On other occasions, children became engaged because of what an adult was doing. For example, in one setting, a woodwork bench was set up in a place where adults were working with children. A number of children were drawn to the activity, possibly because adults were there, although it is also possible that children were drawn to it because of the comparatively novel nature of some of the resources and equipment, such as saws and screwdrivers.

This may be very important for practice. Exploration, having an interest in taking an idea or activity forward, and knowing what you want to do, are aspects of behaviour which, by their nature, occur most often at the beginning of children's engagement in an activity. They serve as conditions, even as 'gatekeepers' for children's on-going involvement and persistence. Interestingly, previous research by Hutt et al. (1989) found that gender was an important dimension of this aspect of initial engagement, with girls in their study more frequently opting for an activity at which an adult was present. The FRF project did not find this, and both boys and girls alike showed their keenness to explore and engage when adults were involved in an activity.

Involvement

Looking at choice and involvement, one of our three categories of creative thinking in the ACCT Framework, Laevers (2000) believes that a key factor in supporting higher levels of involvement (seen by him as an indicator of children's 'intense mental activity') is the opportunities children have for choice: 'the more children can choose their own activities, the higher will be their level of involvement' (2000: 26). Siraj-Blatchford et al. (2002: 12) also suggest that 'freely chosen play activities often provide the best opportunities to extend children's thinking'. In the FRF project, we reached the same conclusion, and our observations showed that child-initiated activities were much more likely to feature the highest levels of children's involvement, particularly in comparison to activities led by adults. In child-initiated activities, children were more likely to involve others and to display more flexibility and originality, imagining and hypothesizing, and analysing their ideas and speculating.

Case study: Involvement in child-initiated activity

Playing outdoors, Gee (age 4.4) has balanced a plank on a milk crate, and has placed a dinosaur model on one end. He begins by using his arms to push one end of the plank down, when another boy comes along and kicks the end. He sees this, and begins using his feet to stamp on the plank. Squatting down, he balances the plank, sliding it so that a longer end is hanging from one side. He seems to assess this, and continues sliding the plank until it is no longer balanced, and starts to tip to the ground. He then slides it back a little until it is balanced. He stamps, but the dinosaur does not go up so high. He turns, looks around: 'Ho!' and smiles broadly.

Rishi (age 3.6) has been watching Gee. He brings a much larger dinosaur which he places on the other end of the plank. Gee takes his dinosaur off, stamps, and the big dinosaur flies through the air and lands near his feet. He quickly places his dinosaur on the other end, and stamps hard. Rishi crawls along to retrieve his dinosaur. He holds the plank down but does not seem to know how to balance it, and it swings up and down as he tries to place his dinosaur on one end. Gee watches, then slides the plank along to balance it. Rishi pulls it back again. Gee stamps on the end of the plank, the dinosaur flies up a little way and lands. Gee then places his dinosaur on one end, while Rishi puts his on the other.

Gee shows evidence of all aspects of involvement, as he tries out and analyses ideas, speculates and involves others. There is also clear evidence of persistence, the third category in the ACCT Framework.

The social context of creative thinking: involvement and enjoyment

In the FRF project, we observed that children were more likely to try out and analyse new ideas when adults were not present. What seems to be important is the presence of play companions. Children showed much more involvement in an activity when they were playing in a group than when they were playing alone: high levels of involvement in the children were observed in over three-quarters of the episodes of group play.

Pair play between friends was also a strong context for supporting the children's involvement, with about 60 per cent of the episodes of pair play having high levels of involvement, in contrast to solitary play, for which only half of the episodes supported such high levels. Friendship may be an important element here (as in the case study of Sapphire and Amanda, on p. 103), as friends are more likely to succeed in problem-solving activities than non-friends (Smith et al., 2003). In the RDs, children often referred to the presence of friends as important. Some children also talked about *not* wanting to play with children that they did not count as friends, and the impact this had on their choices of activity.

Interestingly, children were more likely to be receptive to other ideas and to incorporate them in their thinking and action when these came from an adult, rather than from another child. All of the adults in our study were skilful in encouraging children to make use of prior knowledge, such as reminding them of how to use specific resources, or of ways of doing things. However, we found that, of all adults, teachers were most successful in supporting children in gaining new knowledge, which is a vital aspect of any creative thinking, as shown in the case study on adult support. The EPPE study (Sylva et al., 2010) shows a strong association between high quality provision and appropriately trained and well qualified staff.

 Case study: Adult support

Anna, a teacher, and Catherine, a visiting artist, are engaged in the same woodwork activity. Anna's professional training and experience play a part in her awareness of the value of open-ended, speculative talk, and of the modelling of enquiry, in her support for Zak. Catherine, whilst supportive to Mimi, uses a more directive, didactic approach:

Zak and Teacher Anna:

Zak is holding the hammer with the ball end facing the nail, not the flat end.

Anna: 'I wonder if it works on that side?' Zak turns hammer over ...

Zak hits the nail with the hammer, whilst Anna holds nail in position. Zak pulls Anna's hand away.

Anna: (moving her hand away) 'Oh! If I let go, it's going to fall over!'

Mimi and Artist Catherine:

Mimi picks up the hammer and hits the nail with ball end.

Catherine: (pointing to flat end of hammerhead) 'Bash it with this end' (turns hammerhead over) 'Bash the nail in there ...'

(later) Mimi is turning the screwdriver anticlockwise on screw head.

Catherine: 'Turn it the other way, look, this way' (demonstrating).

Why might this matter? As we saw in Chapter 3, the attitudes of significant adults can either encourage or inhibit children's creative thinking. Whilst making use of prior knowledge is valuable, Vygotsky's (1978: 87) famous statement that 'What a child can do with assistance today she will be able to do by herself tomorrow' emphasizes the value of the acquisition of new knowledge and insights, gained through joint thinking. Siraj-Blatchford et al. (2002: 47) suggest that adult interventions in the most effective settings in their study 'were most often in the form of questions that provoke speculation and extend the imagination'.

The least frequently observed areas of involvement, whether or not adults were present, were children's speculative comments and analysis of their own and others' ideas. During the activities themselves, adults were more successful at engaging children in such thinking than peers, but, interestingly, this kind of thinking often emerged much more in the RDs, with children reflecting on why something had or had not worked: 'He's too big and he's going to fall over me', or 'They've done it all wrong'. It may be that adult support in focusing on talk and reflection is a more powerful means of supporting these aspects of creative thinking.

Persistence: not just a matter of time

The final category in the ACCT Framework focuses on children's persistence and resilience, their ability to sustain their involvement in the face of challenge, and their willingness to take risks and learn from mistakes. These dispositions will also have an impact upon children's sense of self-efficacy, and pleasure in completing challenges, as well as supporting deeper understanding and more complex knowledge (Lambert, 2000). Persistence, though, is not just a matter of how long a child remains involved in an activity. Whilst some episodes observed in the FRF project were very long, children's persistence in the face of difficulty and challenge, and sense of self-efficacy, was also present in short activities. Again, this was most evident in child-initiated activities, and activities in which practitioners were absent. All 10 episodes with the highest levels of persistence in children were child-initiated, and in nine of these, practitioners were absent. It could be that practitioners are victims of their own skill to some extent: in planning adult-directed or adult-led activities that are skilfully matched to the children's competences, they may present the children with fewer problems or risks with which they must deal. In child-initiated activities in which adults are not present, it may be that the interventions of peers are more likely to result in challenges and problems which a child must overcome.

An important implication for practice is the comparative absence of risk-taking behaviour in the children. Tovey (2007) identifies positive links between risk-taking and key areas of children's learning. These include the assessment and management of risk as a survival skill, a sense of mastery, and children's emotional well-being and resilience. Shared understanding between practitioners in a setting involving risk-taking, along with the confidence to support children in taking risks, are important, and activities such as the woodwork in the 'Adult support' case study are valuable contexts for encouraging this. In addition, the greater (albeit still relatively low) frequency of risk-taking behaviour in child-initiated activities in which adults were absent may be because children support and encourage one another more in taking risks in their play. This emphasizes the value of practitioners looking at ways to support this in their planning and interactions with children.

An understanding that not all risks are physical ones, like using woodwork tools or climbing and balancing, is an important implication for practice. Angelique (age 3.6) showed clearly that she felt a sense of 'permission' to take risks, and of learning from mistakes when she painted her hands and used them to stick pieces of foil onto her painting, when conventional glue and spreader did not work.

The RDs often proved to be important in revealing how children saw themselves. Chloe (age 4.6), for example, commented that she had chosen to draw a house because 'I'm good at them'. Looking at her finished picture on the video, she said, 'Ah, I think it was perfect'. The children's sense of themselves as thinkers was also often most evident in the RDs, with children commenting on their own ideas and those of others: '… and then I had a good idea', or 'It wasn't my idea, it was Amy's'.

Creative thinking: looking at some activities

As we have already said, all types of activity, both 'creative' and otherwise, can be strong contexts for supporting young children's creative thinking. However, some activities may potentially afford children more opportunities than others. One such activity is pretend play. The evidence from the FRF project reflected some of the ideas discussed in Chapter 3 about the value of pretend play for creative and flexible thinking (Singer, 1973). Pretend play, particularly socio-dramatic play, was the most likely of any activity in the FRF project to lead to high levels of creative thinking. A comparison of episodes of pretence and episodes of 'creative' activities showed similar frequencies of 'trying out ideas', particularly through imagining and hypothesizing. But the activities involving shared pretence had much higher incidences of 'involving others', especially in articulating ideas and persuading others. Much pretend play, particularly in this age group, is collaborative: providing a context for children to engage with others, hypothesizing about their wishes and intentions as they negotiate story lines, and imagining how co-players will feel, think and act, as in the case study of Sapphire and Amanda.

Case study: Pretend play, friendship and involvement

Two friends, Sapphire (age 4.2) and Amanda (age 3.9) try out and analyse their ideas, imagine and hypothesize and negotiate roles in their socio-dramatic play.

Sapphire: This is for baby, bibs are for babies (she has difficulty fitting it on the doll's neck, and takes it off and puts it on the floor). That doesn't work, that one (Amanda bends down, picks it up and holds it out). No, that is for babies.

Amanda: This one?

Sapphire: That's your bib and this one is a baby's bib.

Amanda: You know what, I don't have a baby.

Sapphire: No, you are the little baby and I am your mummy and this is your little sister. You are the big baby and this is your little sister.

Amanda: (crouching down) Pretend I'm the little 2-year-old baby. (Sapphire nods and Amanda puts her hand on Sapphire's arm.)

Sapphire: (smiling) No, you say goo goo.

Amanda: But I say baby words.

Sapphire: This is your little sister (folds bib and puts it in box, beside doll).

Exploring materials

Children's exploratory play with materials and resources of all kinds provided a very strong context for their creative thinking. For example, Ella (age 4.6) spent much of one afternoon using a digital camera. She explored what the camera itself could do, pressing buttons and observing the lens extend, and taking pictures and looking at them on the camera screen. She also focused on seeing what she could do with the camera, as she held it out in front of her, watching the image change on the screen as she walked across the nursery with it, or as she used it to 'see' underneath the climbing frame, pointing it upwards. She involved others, asking them to 'say cheese' as she took their photographs, and showed them the results on screen. In talking later about this in the RD, Ella told her keyperson, Samantha, that she had wanted to take pictures of her friend Chloe's eyes, which she then loaded onto the computer to look at, and printed out to display on the nursery wall.

Some of the richest examples of young children's creative thinking came from their novel or unexpected ways of using materials. Jagdish (age 3.8) discovered he could pick pencils up in the open jaws of a pair of scissors, and spent considerable time transporting every pen and pencil from one side of the table to the other, and picking up stray pencils from the floor. As he did so, he tried out ideas – does a 'snipping' action with the scissors work better than keeping them still, for example? – and analysed them – when one pencil rolled across the table he first tried moving it back with his hand, and then decided that resting it against the side of a roll of tape would keep it still whilst he manoeuvred the scissors open. He persisted until he had completed his self-set task, showing confidence and a sense of self-efficacy. Similarly, Jake (age 4.6) decided that a more interesting use for masking tape was both winding it round himself (involving much analysis of how long a piece of tape was needed, how this could be measured around your head when you cannot see the back of your head, and how to use scissors in such circumstances), and then around the legs and seat of his chair. Again, it is children's sense of permission to use materials in different ways which is important here, and this is facilitated by adults' openness to children's thinking.

Playing outdoors

One significant aspect of young children's choice of activity and its success as a context for their creative thinking was the use of outdoors. The vast majority of outdoor play we recorded showed high levels of children's creative thinking behaviour, whether this was alone or with others, and regardless of adult presence or absence. Some of these episodes involved activities unique to outdoors – digging and gardening, for example – whilst others were activities that could also have occurred inside, such as pretence and construction. As we noted in Chapter 3, it may be that outdoors affords children time and space to think creatively, and facilitates a greater range of creative responses (Compton et al., 2010).

Conclusion

To conclude this chapter, it is valuable to highlight eight significant implications of the findings from the study that used the ACCT Framework:

- Adults play a particularly important role in supporting children's initial engagement in activities;

- The highest levels of children's involvement in activities, and the most frequent expressions of creative thinking, occur in child-initiated activities;

- Playing in a group, or in a friendship pair, may be particularly valuable in promoting children's involvement in activities;

- Adult scaffolding, using open-ended questions, speculation and modelling enquiry, may be especially valuable for supporting children in acquiring new knowledge, developing new skills, and making use of these in support of their creative thinking;

- Dialogue between adults and children may be especially valuable for supporting children's analysis of their ideas and activities, and for their reflections on themselves as thinkers;

- Pretend play is particularly valuable for supporting creative thinking;

- Children's opportunities to explore materials and ideas, and to use resources in novel, unexpected ways, support the development of their creative thinking;

- Outdoors is a powerful context for supporting young children's creative thinking.

 Reflection

Look back at the ACCT Framework in Table 8.1:

- What examples could you include here from your own experience?

- 'Analysing ideas' and 'risk taking' were the two least frequently observed aspects of creative thinking in the FRF project. Why, in your view, might this be? What could you do to support young children in these areas?

Parents' experiences of supporting young children's creative thinking

Sue Greenfield

This chapter focuses on:

- The ways in which parents view their relationship with practitioners;
- The value of using video-recorded episodes during home visits to parents;
- Parents' perceptions of what children do at home and their understanding of creative thinking;
- Parents' interpretation of the connections between what children do at home and in the early childhood setting.

The value of parental involvement in settings and the importance of parents' role in their children's learning both at home and at school, has been discussed in Chapters 4 and 6. The premise that 'what parents do' with their children is more important than 'who parents are' (Sylva et al., 2004), as well as the emphasis placed on parental involvement by government policy (e.g. DCSF, 2008; DfE, 2011), has provided encouragement to practitioners to include all parents in their children's learning, and, by implication, in their creative thinking. In these earlier chapters we discussed not only the importance of the relationships between practitioners and families, but also the association between parental involvement and children's social and cognitive development.

It is evident that involving parents in any way is no easy task (e.g. MacNaughton and Hughes, 2011; Whalley and the Pen Green Centre Team, 2007). The formation of partnerships in which both parents and practitioners are able to develop mutual understandings of each other and exchange knowledge and ideas about children can be achieved (e.g. Draper and Wheeler, 2010), but requires skill on the part of the practitioners. Relationships have to move from initial superficiality to the involvement not only of mutual understanding, but also of listening skills, respect and empathy. This is not to say that children should take part in the same activities in the settings and at home, but rather that home and setting should have an idea of their own and each other's interpretations and priorities for children's learning (Chapters 4 and 10). Our premise is that all parents whose children attend early years settings should have some relationship with those settings, although that these may not always develop beyond superficiality.

Practitioners are provided with many challenges as they strive to form relationships with all parents in their settings, and try to enable partnerships in which both partners can contribute knowledge about the children. This chapter focuses on these relationships from the parents' understanding of their partnerships with settings, and of their children's creative thinking. As discussed in Chapter 6, the FRF project evidence was obtained by discussing video examples of their children's creative thinking with parents at home. We made the assumption that parents would be more comfortable to discuss their children's learning, and the ways in which they work with the practitioners, in their own homes. All the parents had an interest in their children's learning, and this was demonstrated by the strength of their requests to know more about 'what he/she *really* does at nursery'. One mother gave a description of how she would 'tiptoe round the fence to see what he was doing outside in the [nursery] garden'.

Parents' views of their relationships with practitioners

Perceptions of the nursery

Most of the parents interviewed made positive comments about the nurseries their children attended:

> *It definitely made a difference him going to nursery. He loves it there.*

This is typical of many of the comments about the parents' overviews of the settings. Another parent said:

> *I'm very happy with the nursery. I'm probably pushy but I ask questions if*

I have them. I go in and ask staff and they don't seem to mind.

It was clear that parents thought that their children had gained many advantages from their attendance at nursery. This is particularly interesting because, as we shall discuss later, they had little idea of what their children did at nursery, yet were nevertheless able to see that their children had progressed.

Time

Parents, in general, seem to have an impression that practitioners have little time available to communicate with them. As we see in Chapter 10, time, and the way it is used, is an issue for practitioners who wish to spend more time with the children, and this also applies to the time practitioners spend with parents. This tension is highlighted in a study by Martin (2003), who draws attention to the fact that many parents felt that the staff did not have enough time available to form trusting relationships with them. The parents in the FRF project suggested that the lack of time to communicate with practitioners was also a problem for them. One parent who worked with young children in another setting said:

> *I know how hard it is to make time to speak to the parents. If only teachers could tell us … There is just no time … not when you've got 30-odd kids.*

All of the parents interviewed suggested that practitioners' perceived hurry and lack of time deterred them from becoming involved in conversation. They did not feel able to gain as much information about their children as they required. MacNaughton and Hughes (2011) suggest that in parent–practitioner relationships, lack of time can be used as a means of 'silencing parents and vice versa' (2011: 6). For example, practitioners are often particularly busy when children are being dropped off or collected, and this reduces communication to a minimum. Parents perceive that practitioners are busy, and this 'silences' some parents who may have wanted to discuss their children, particularly those who are not confident (e.g. those for whom English is not their first language). These parents often need time and space to feel confident to communicate, and this is not evidently available in many settings. Some parents were happy with the ways in which they were able to interact with practitioners, but others suggested that nobody communicated unless there was 'a problem'.

> *They [the practitioners] don't have time to talk. The only time they'll speak is when there's been a problem. They don't really say nothing.*

Time was an issue for parents in a different way when they had made an appointment to discuss their children's progress with practitioners. In one setting in our project, comprehensive reports had been written about the children, including detailed information about their learning, social skills and general development. Parents were given appointments to discuss these reports, but some parents found them difficult to understand. For example, one parent said:

> ... when I had the meeting at the end of year report type thing ... it was very quick, going through it was all very quick. The time they've given to discuss this with parents and what it means is all very quick.

And another parent:

> My English is not good. I have this [the report of progress]. I don't understand ... no time, teacher have no time. My English is not good.

These parents did not feel comfortable about asking questions or asking for clarification, as they felt this would have taken up too much of the practitioners' time. They saw that the practitioners were very busy and that their time was limited, so they remained quiet and did not ask anything. We do not know whether the practitioners were aware of the parents' lack of confidence, but their silence could have been construed as parents' lack of interest in their children. What is certain is that these parents left the meeting about their children's progress with very little information. The reports must have taken practitioners a long time to prepare, and they must have had the intention of developing trusting relationships with the parents, and to involve them in children's education (e.g. Knofp and Swick, 2008; Morrow and Malin, 2004). Yet, unfortunately, many practitioners may have taken for granted that these families would understand what was meant by such phrases as; 'conservation of number' or 'cause and effect'.

There is further discussion in Chapter 10 about the burden that has been placed on practitioners regarding written evidence. The comments made by these parents highlight the fact that because of their lack of time, the practitioners had not been able to develop a 'comprehensive understanding of families and the issues involved when working with them' (Baum and Swick, 2008). It strongly suggests that there is a need to reflect on the ways in which reports are written so that they form the basis of discussion between the parents and the practitioners.

Trusting relationships between parents and practitioners

Over the years, many authors have discussed the issue of trust between parents and practitioners (e.g. Ball, 1994; Draper and Wheeler, 2010; Pugh and De'Ath, 1989), and it is one of the most problematic aspects of any partnership, whether it is between parents and practitioners or the relationships between different agencies working together with children (Greenfield, 2010b). In the FRF project, several parents described instances in which they felt that the practitioners did not 'believe' them. For instance, one father related how he had been asked to practise sequencing with his daughter at home using a set of picture cards:

> *I told them: 'she can do that now', but I know they didn't believe me. Then the next week they said I must've practised because she could do it so well. I hadn't done nothing at home but I didn't tell them that.*

Another parent who at first said that her relationship with staff was good, demonstrated her lack of trust when she said:

> *Even when the teachers say 'Yeah they do this and they do that', you still think in the back of your mind: 'but do they?' I was getting like really concerned that he doesn't get along with the other kids ... but seeing this [the video clip of his play episodes in the setting] is really surprising. He's actually ... he's playing with other kids!*

This highlights the parent's anxiety about her son in a place she seems to know little about, although her lack of trust in the staff and her anxiety may have been alleviated by seeing the video clip.

For practitioners, it can be a challenge to develop trusting relationships with all parents. Trust between practitioners and parents may seem to exist on the surface, but once the relationship is scrutinized, the existence of trust can be questionable. However, many authors have discussed the ways in which trusting relationships between parents and practitioners can be developed through training. For instance at the Pen Green Centre for Children and their Families in England, practitioners have developed the use of a 'shared language' with parents to assist them in discussing the ways in which children learn and develop, and to foster the development of trust between them (Whalley and the Pen Green Centre Team, 2007: 132). Draper and Wheeler (2010) suggest that the PEAL (Parents and Early Learning: http://peal.org.uk) training for staff and parents provides a means for both to gain mutual understanding, and the Family Partnership Model (Davis et al., 2002) provides training to enable families and practitioners to work together collaboratively. Practitioners are beginning to have a clearer understanding of the importance of parental involvement; however, it can still be a challenge to make use of the understanding gained in these training programmes in practice, especially as they increasingly work with children and families from diverse social and cultural backgrounds (see Chapters 4 and 10).

Case study: misunderstandings

Archie, a 3-year-old, attends a maintained nursery school in Inner London. His mum says that she is very pleased with his progress since he began nursery:

> He is so happy to go there every day and it means I have some time with this one (Archie's baby sister) on her own. He gets bored in the holidays and keeps asking 'is it nursery today?'.

Archie's mum watches the DVD of her son at nursery. She watches Archie who hovers at the edge of a group of children, watching, as they attempt to build a brick wall. After a while, a practitioner who has also been watching the group, speaks to Archie and invites him to take part. He puts on the 'workman gloves' and joins his peers. Archie's mum says:

> Oh! That is so good. I have taught him that the most important thing to remember is he must wait his turn. He really is waiting, isn't he? I'm so pleased!

To observers, it looked as though Archie was a very timid boy who was happy to observe rather than to take part, but the insight from his mother about what she has been teaching him puts a different slant on what is happening here.

Discuss:

- How might the view of the parent about priorities for Archie's development differ from the view of practitioners?

- What could be done to help the development of mutual understanding between the parents and the practitioners?

- Have you come across any instances like this?

The benefit of using video-recorded play episodes with parents in their own homes

The use of video-recorded play episodes of children in the FRF project has already been discussed in Chapter 5. One of the benefits regarding the involvement of parents in the project was the recruitment of the participants. The parents were asked to volunteer to take part and many of them did so because they wanted the opportunity to watch the video of their child so that they could 'see what they really do at school'.

Flewitt (2006) discusses the ways in which the perceptions of the adults in her study differ for the same children in different social situations. In the

FRF project, some parents' first comments after watching the video clips were concerned with the difference between their children's behaviour at home and in the setting. After watching the DVD, one mother said:

> *No. (pointing to video) That's not Matthew, not at all. He's always got children telling him what to do. He don't play on his own. Matthew ... he'll try something once and if it goes wrong he won't go back and do it again he just walks away. Yet here he's completely different.*

Practitioners commented that, at nursery, Matthew was often seen to be a leader, as the video clip showed, but his mother found it very difficult to believe that the confident child on the screen was her son. He was the youngest of four, and at home, he let others speak for him and rarely completed any task. As Flewitt (2006) suggests, using video material provides a multi-modal means of viewing young children's learning so that a much more complete picture of the child can be provided. If Matthew's mother had been told that her child was confident or that he was happy to take the lead in activities with other children, she may have been reluctant to believe it. Now she was able to view his behaviour at nursery as many times as she wanted, and could begin to complete her knowledge and understanding of his learning and to celebrate the progress he was making. It enabled her to follow this up at home with a much more positive view of her son's abilities.

In another example at a different setting, Annie, a 3-year-old, surprised her mother:

> *It really surprised me. Annie was quite quiet. Jodie was more bossy than her. At home, she [Annie] likes to be in charge of everything ... erm if she wants something, she tends to get her own way. She's very like that. She's very strong minded. She never wants us to help her. She wants to work things out for herself.*

Several parents were surprised by their children's concentration and perseverance at a task, and commented:

> *He's been doing that for ages. He's not like that at home. He gets bored.*

> *I'm surprised he's been doing this for quite long ... normally he seems to have ... a short attention span.*

These parents were provided with the visual image to complete the pictures they had of their children in a way that would not have been possible using written reports or the words of the practitioners. They were delighted to see their children who often claimed they did 'nothing' at nursery, happily taking part in activities. The video material can provide a starting point for some meaningful dialogue between practitioners and parents that would help them begin the 'nurturance of an involvement process', which is so important for their mutual understanding of the children (Swick, 2007: 100). Though parents had seen longer video clips of all the children in the nursery from time to time, they had never been given the opportunity to watch a clip that focused on their own children, and had the chance to discuss this with the practitioner. The parents in the FRF project were very happy that they could begin to know 'what he/she *really does at nursery*'.

Parents' perceptions of what children do at home and their understanding of creative thinking

Hannon et al. (2006) suggest that there is very little research into parents' views of how they promote children's literacy at home. In the same way, parents' understanding of children's creative thinking, and how this may be fostered at home, has seldom been addressed by researchers. This is surprising when others (e.g. Draper and Wheeler, 2010; Sammons et al., 2007) discuss the increasing awareness of the importance of the home learning environment in providing activities to encourage children's thinking and development. In Chapter 4 we have discussed the diversity of the ways in which children express their creative thinking, and the various ways in which parents support this process. As discussed in Chapter 6, home visits can provide insights into the lives of the families as well as into the relationships between parents and children that may not be observed in the early childhood settings. There is no doubt that the parents interviewed had insight into their children's activities, even though they sometimes found it difficult to express this clearly.

What children do at home

At first, parents were reticent about providing details of the activities their children enjoyed at home. Some of them clearly outlined the importance of reading and writing, especially those for whom school entry was imminent. One mother spoke of the '*need to get Jenny up to speed with reading and writing*' and several commented on the fact that their children were '*never happy to do any reading or writing*'.

When asked about creative thinking, parents usually described the kind of activities that are most likely to be considered creative such as mark making, music, dance that we discussed in Chapter 8. When asked what their children liked doing at home, parents made comments such as: '*he's very imaginative*', '*she's always singing and dancing*' or '*he loves doing bits of reading and writing*'. Interestingly, the video clips show very different activities to these. After watching the recordings of their children's play episodes at nursery, I asked: 'What does ... like to do at home?'. This time they divulged much more detailed information such as: '*football*', '*fighting with her brothers and sisters'*, *'making me miserable'* and *'cutting up my bed sheet into little pieces'*, and insisted the nursery should not know about these endeavours. They had never mentioned them to the practitioners as they probably did not want the practitioners to misunderstand their children or view them in negative ways. There were also comments made by parents that provided an insight into the children's learning. For instance, one mother said:

> *Every week he'll play with something different and he'll play with something every day until he's bored. When he's bored … he'll stop. He won't play with it again until one day, he'll think: 'I haven't played with it for ages.' He investigates everything.*

This mother realizes that his enjoyment of 'investigating' is an important part of his development, and suggests that creative thinking may well be involved in the investigation. Though all parents included in the FRF project were unsure about what creative thinking might be, they all provided instances of their children's creative thinking at home. For instance, Ed's parents talked about his pretend play:

Dad: I've noticed he [Ed] does things for quite long now.

Mum: Yeah, he does sit with things … in the bath.

Dad: And nowadays, what I noticed, even last night he's in there a lot longer, playing with his toys and that. We were listening to him yesterday playing with his toys in the bath: (*imitating Ed's voice*) 'OK you're under the water. You need help! I'll get some help! I'll get some help!'

Mum: You could hear he's really playing now. He makes up stories with those men.

Dad: At first we wondered what it was all about but you should hear his stories!

Ed's parents had never spoken to practitioners about this though it was obvious that they valued the way their son was progressing. Many of the parent interviews showed similar understanding about the importance of pretend play. They also discussed exploration and investigation as significant in fostering children's creative thinking.

Many parents made it clear that the children's attendance at nursery partly contributed to their children's progress, but had said nothing about this to the nursery. This is disappointing for two reasons. Firstly, practitioners would have also valued what parents noticed about children's progress at home, and this may have provided opportunities for establishing shared understanding about children. Secondly, such information provided by the parents could have been used by practitioners to support children's creative thinking at nursery, and strengthen the relationship between home and the setting. As Knopf and Swick (2007: 291) maintain, 'many early childhood educators find it extremely difficult to facilitate parent involvement at levels that will result in significant change [in children's academic achievement]'. The lack of communication between parents and practitioners is problematic as they would both miss the opportunities to learn about the children, and to foster the ways in which they support children's creative thinking. It seems clear that if 'what parents do at home' is important (Sylva et al., 2010), then further emphasis needs to be placed on the relationship between home and setting, and for practitioners to set this as a priority.

Conclusion

There are several significant conclusions to be reached and these are outlined below.

- To achieve parent partnership remains a challenge for many early childhood settings: the FRF project suggests that further efforts need to be made in order to support parents to feel comfortable about exchanging information with practitioners.

- Written information and reports on children's progress are not always understood by the parents. There is a strong need for practitioners to make time to provide one-to-one feedback about children's experiences in the setting, and to listen to parents' concerns on a more regular basis.

- Many parents seem lacking in confidence about the large amount of knowledge that they have concerning their own children, and the ways in which they value their children's activities at home. Further encouragement and support for parents are needed to help them gain in confidence in promoting their children's creative thinking at home.

- Many parents in the FRF project value children's reading and writing more than many other activities taking place at home. If practitioners were to communicate the importance of children's creative thinking, activities suggested in the *Analysis of Young Children's Creative Thinking* Framework (Chapters 3, 5 and 8) should be shared with parents.

- The use of visual images of children's activities in the nurseries has been helpful for parents to understand what their children do in these settings. Bearing in mind that the usage of video recording in settings can be complex (see Chapters 3, 5 and 8), it can greatly promote communication between parents and practitioners. This is especially the case for those parents who have limited experience with English language and culture.

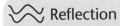 Reflection

If you are a practitioner:

- How do you communicate children's activities at early childhood settings to parents? Do you feel that parents understand what you communicate to them?
- Think of the parents in your setting. Do you feel that you have trusting relationships with them? Are you concerned about the ways in which you communicate with some parents?
- In your setting, do you make use of video recordings and other visual materials to communicate with parents? If so, in what ways do you use them? If not, why not?

If you are a researcher:

- Design a study that elicits parents' understanding of children's creative thinking by taking into consideration the points discussed in this chapter.

10

Practitioners' experiences of promoting children's creative thinking

Hiroko Fumoto

This chapter focuses on:

- The challenges in everyday practice that practitioners face in promoting children's creative thinking;

- The attributes that practitioners bring to their practice that are likely to play a significant role in promoting children's creative thinking;

- The implications of these challenges and attributes for policy, professional development, and research.

The question of how practitioners can best promote children's creative thinking has attracted much attention from political, practical and research perspectives, as we have seen. A proliferation of literature provides practical tips and advice to practitioners on how to enhance children's creativity (e.g. Connors, 2010). As Sternberg (2008) suggests, we want children (and adults) to exercise 'the creative skills used to generate excellent ideas, the practical skills used to implement those ideas, and the wisdom to be able to discern how to make a positive difference in the world' (2008: 150). The role played by practitioners in this is considerable. It includes their 'sensitive engagement with children and with their families' (Craft, 2008: 96); valuing children's 'agency' (2008: 99); sustaining children's engagement with tasks through teaching them 'appropriate

119

technical skills and a secure knowledge base' (Prentice, 2000: 155); and promoting their 'cultural curiosity' (2000: 156). The importance of facilitating a disposition towards thinking in creative ways has also been noted by many authors (e.g. Cremin et al., 2006; Duffy, 2009). As we have argued throughout the book, the social environment that promotes children's intrinsic motivation is also crucial for the development of creativity (Hennessey, 2003). In particular, we have highlighted the importance of communicative relationships between practitioners, children and their parents in influencing this process (see Chapter 4).

In practice, though, how do practitioners experience their roles of promoting children's creative thinking? This chapter addresses this question in an effort to shed further light on the complexity of promoting children's creative thinking within their everyday interactions with children and parents. The discussion is based on two main premises:

- As the expression of children's creative thinking is multifaceted, so too are the ways in which practitioners promote this in their practice (Chapter 4). For instance, whilst there are similarities, it is likely that practitioners in Japan interact with children differently from their counterparts in England. It is equally likely that there is diversity of practice within a particular culture.

- Given our focus on children's everyday creativity (Chapters 2, 3 and 4), there are many challenges and issues that are shared by practitioners worldwide.

Challenges in everyday practice

There are several challenges inherent in early childhood practice that have direct or indirect effects on the ways in which practitioners promote children's creative thinking. These include issues concerning practitioners' pay and conditions, the training of the workforce, the resourcing of early childhood provision, and practitioners' professionalization (e.g. Miller, 2008; Moloney, 2010; Urban, 2008). These are likely, to varying degrees, to influence practitioners' experiences of the ways in which they work with children and their families (see Lerner, 2002). There are also four other challenges that are particularly relevant to the promotion of children's creative thinking, which are dealt with in the next four sections.

Time to be with children

Despite the importance to practitioners of developing communicative relationships with children and encouraging their creative disposition, they express concerns about the apparent lack of time for them to be with children during sessions in early childhood settings. In England, for instance, the pressure on time seems to be keenly felt by many practitioners because of the increasing requirements for record-keeping and paperwork, which they often experience as 'political interference and ideology', as Siraj-Blatchford recorded in 1993. Nearly two decades later, the situation remains the same, if not even worse, as demonstrated in Brooker et al.'s (2010) examination of practitioners' experience of the *Early Years Foundation Stage* (DfES, 2007). Practitioners are generally in favour of the EYFS and the impact it has had on their practice, but they have also raised some concerns, such as:

> [the] time taken for paperwork, and for observing and collecting evidence; challenges resulting from changes in ratio as children become older; associated difficulties over transitions within and beyond the EYFS; and some of the rules and regulations which are experienced as excessive. (Brooker et al., 2010: 78)

The importance of monitoring and recording children's experiences is recognized by all practitioners, and Brooker et al.'s study also draws a complex picture of the ways in which factors such as pay and conditions and practitioners' training backgrounds may influence how they deal with the demands placed upon them. Yet the message seems clear: that 'the demand for written evidence [has become] excessive and that this [is taking] valuable time away from their work with the children' (Brooker et al., 2010: 79). The Tickell Review of the EYFS (DfE, 2011) clearly identifies the need to 'simplify' the EYFS Profile and 'to reduce the burden that paperwork introduces' to practitioners (DfE, 2011: 30). This is a welcome step forward, although the simplification of the record keeping should not compromise the quality of the observations that practitioners make in their practice.

In contrast, practitioners in the USA seem to be facing a different kind of pressure on their time to be with children. They are confronting the issue of accountability and its effect on their day-to-day practice. Miller and Almon (2009), in their *Crisis in the Kindergarten: Why Children Need to Play in School*, discuss the 'out-of-control testing' (2009: 39) in which standardized tests are being used in an attempt to improve the education system. They are concerned that testing leads to a decline in the children's opportunities to play and to express their creative thinking. Hirsh-Pasek et al. (2009), Gopnik (2009) and the National Association for the Education of Young Children (NAEYC) (2009) all concur with this view, and argue for the need to bring back playful learning in early childhood settings.

The implications of this pressurized environment for practice can be far-reaching. For instance, if there is an apparent lack of time for practitioners to be with children, does this correspondingly reduce the time available to develop meaningful relationships with parents (Chapter 9)? In what way might a culture of 'standard overload' (NAEYC, 2009) influence practitioners' relationships with children and parents? Do many practitioners feel that they are no longer in control of their work? And how might the lack of time to engage in 'Sustained-Shared Thinking' (Siraj-Blatchford,

2010a) with children affect their learning and well-being? (see Fumoto and Robson, 2006 for further discussion).

Meeting the individual needs of children within a group

The understanding of each child's interests and the opportunity to listen to his/her thoughts and ideas have been highlighted as important aspects of the ways in which practitioners promote children's creative thinking. The challenge is for them to do so whilst working with children in groups. This may have become one of the most undermined areas of practitioners' work, as the focus on meeting the individual needs of children and their families seems to have intensified over the years, at least in many industrialized societies. This is not to say that the individual needs of children should not take precedence over the needs of a group, but the challenge for practitioners is to balance these needs in their everyday practice. Some of the practitioners' comments from the FRF project and its related studies succinctly illustrate their concerns. For instance, a practitioner working in a Children's Centre commented on her interactions with a 4-year-old boy:

> *I probably need to bring him into activities a bit more and extend him in different areas ... find out exactly where he is at. I've been trying to do observations on him but I haven't got around to doing it, as I said, because the other children are quite demanding around me. They all need a lot of reassurance ...*

Other practitioners also voiced concerns about how they are finding it physically difficult to interact with each child during sessions on a regular basis:

> *... it would be nice to do the focused activity with every child but there isn't just the time with all the other pressures you have. We try to get around and see as many children as possible but just can't do it.*

> *So the only time I get to do it [e.g. sustained-shared thinking] is maybe on a Wednesday which is my focused activity day ... which is the day I'm allowed to ... that I can just tune into the children. For me, that day is like, definitely the reason why I've taken on this job.*

> *Sometimes you feel like you're not doing enough for them because there are just so many children and you feel like you want to do more.*

These comments indicate practitioners' frustration at not being able to engage in meaningful interactions with children as often as they want to. There is also the issue of monitoring for safety when working with a group of children, as one of the practitioners commented:

> *... you are monitoring more for their safety rather than sitting down and doing what you have to do with them.*

 Case study

Susan works in a maintained nursery school in Inner City London in which the children and families that she works with come from culturally and socially diverse backgrounds. When asked about how her school involves parents in their day-to-day practice, she talked about one of the mothers who has been suffering from mental health issues:

> It is a concern for us for her to be with other children, let alone her own child. This year, we are not inviting any parents to come in and work with us because you can't say to one parent: 'We'll have parents in the nursery but sorry we can't have you'.

She went on to talk about another mother:

> Then there was another parent ... she's desperate to get in [to help in the nursery] and we just couldn't ... she didn't want to come for the children. She wanted to come to be with the other adults. Obviously we're here to listen to parents. But we need to be with the children. And it got to the point where we used to have to ask her to leave because she'd be in floods of tears, bawling, or depending on what part of her medication she'd been on that day ... So it just wasn't good for the children for her to be there.

Discuss the ways Susan and her team dealt with the parents. Did she and her colleagues make the right decision in withdrawing the invitation to all parents to come into the nursery to be involved in activities? Could there have been different ways of involving parents, as suggested in Chapter 6? Consider what you might have done in a similar situation.

Cultural and social diversity: knowing, experiencing and practising

Over the years, our awareness of cultural and social diversity has increased tremendously as we are exposed to the lives of other people across the globe through various media and literature. Whilst there is still a long way to go (Chapters 6 and 9), the field of early childhood has also embraced the notion of diversity through socio-cultural theory (e.g. Rogoff, 2003) and Bronfenbrenner's (1979) ecological systems model, amongst others. More and more practitioners are working with families from varied backgrounds, and it is now almost inconceivable not to talk about diversity when considering children's experiences. Furthermore, notions such as 'child-centred' and 'play-based' learning are embedded in cultural interpretation (e.g. Fleer, 2006; Lee and Tseng, 2008), and are slowly but surely gaining ground.

Knowing about cultural and social diversity is one thing, experiencing it is quite another (Baldock, 2010). The challenge is to translate this into practice in the ways in which children's experiences are valued and extended. To take teacher–child relationships as an example, those engaged in working with young children all know that relationships are critical for children's learning and development, and indeed for their well-being. But the process of relating to a group of children can be complex. For instance, when working with children who speak English as an additional language (EAL), research shows that it generally takes longer for teachers to be in tune with these children than with those who can communicate to them in English (Fumoto et al., 2007). Saft and Pianta (2001) also show how teachers in the USA were more likely to rate their relationships positively when children came from the same ethnic background. They suggest that 'congruence of expectations based on ethnic background, perhaps reflecting culture-specific definitions of expectations for children's behavior, plays a significant but small role in shaping teacher perceptions' (Saft and Pianta, 2001: 138). In addition, Chen (2007) demonstrates the ways in which EAL children may be experiencing possible 'linguistic, cultural and educational isolation' (2007: 41) in primary schools in England. Whilst they are much older than the children addressed in this book, the important point is that their sense of isolation and of being at a disadvantage were not understood by their teachers. These children's experiences are likely to have a significant impact on the ways in which they express their creative thinking in the school context.

Another serious challenge is the practitioners' work with parents from diverse backgrounds (Chapters 4, 6 and 9). For instance, one of the practitioners mentioned that 'I don't have a problem with children but I don't think we are the best communicators with EAL parents, and we have quite a lot' (cited in Fumoto et al., 2007). The case study included in this chapter also shows that similar complexities exist for practitioners when working with parents who seem to be suffering from mental health issues. The practitioner in the case study also felt that often, these complexities are not adequately dealt with during various professional development courses. As she indicated, she 'knows' that parental involvement is the key, but the reality presents enormous challenges.

A possible gap between theory and practice

These challenges seem to indicate a possible gap between theory and practice. As Urban (2008: 141) argues, there may exist an 'epistemological hierarchy' in which 'the professional body of knowledge is *produced* (academic research, scholarly debate), *transferred* (professional preparation, pre- and in-service training) and *applied* (practice)'. As we discussed in Chapter 7, an important effort is being made to adopt the 'communities of practice' approach to research by involving practitioners as part of research communities. However, policy, research and practice might still be disjointed for many practitioners, and these may be the ones who are most aware of this gap. This, in turn, could have serious implications for the ways in which they work with children and parents.

Attributes that practitioners bring to their practice

Here, it is useful to draw on developmental systems theory (DST) (Ford and Lerner, 1992) in order to understand how these attributes are likely to play a significant role in promoting children's creative thinking. The main tenet of DST is its emphasis on conceptualizing human development as 'an open, self-regulating and self-constructing system' (Ford and Lerner, 1992: 91). In other words, individuals have the ability to influence their own development to a certain extent by the ways in which they perceive the events and phenomena around them. In particular, the social environment can have a powerful influence on this process as individuals stimulate changes in each other over time, thereby mutually changing the developmental contexts of one another (Lerner, 2002). When this is applied to practitioners' work with children, it can be said that an attribute such as their determination to enhance their practice, and the ways in which they perceive challenges and their relationships with children, can have a significant influence on their practice. Through their relationships with children, their practice can be seen as partially creating the developmental contexts for children and their parents.

There are countless attributes that practitioners bring to their practice. The length of their experience in the field is a case in point. Novice and experienced teachers are likely to perceive their environments differently: but this does not imply that the latter are necessarily more mature in dealing with challenges, as experience on its own can bring complacency. Novice teachers can bring fresh perspectives to the profession. This section focuses on three key themes that have arisen from the FRF project (e.g. Fumoto and Robson, 2006; Robson and Fumoto, 2009), and its related studies (Fumoto, 2005, 2011; Fumoto et al., 2003, 2007). They are overlapping themes that appear to mutually facilitate one another.

Professional autonomy

Having a sense of control over one's work is important in dealing with everyday challenges. Leontiev (2006: 56) explains that autonomy is constituted by the ways individuals 'impose their regulatory principles to the way they manage their lives'. This is closely related to Bandura's notion of self-efficacy, which explains how beliefs about our own capability can influence what we are trying to achieve (Bandura, 1989). In a sense, professional autonomy can be conceptualized as practitioners' beliefs about their ability to take control of various challenges in order to achieve a desired goal, such as a successful promotion of children's creative thinking.

For instance, in the FRF project, we showed how some practitioners were able to take control of their environment by creating a condition that would be likely to promote children's thinking. We found that practitioners who felt that they had enough time during the session to enhance children's thinking were more likely to:

- make time for children to complete activities;

- feel that they have enough time to play with the children and to 'stand back' and observe them;

- provide opportunities for children to make decisions for themselves;

- be confident about the ways in which they were involving parents to support children's thinking (Fumoto and Robson, 2006: 106–7).

In addition, in settings in which practitioners were comfortable in dealing with some of the constraints, they were also confident in applying their own interpretation to EYFS recommendations. They used them to their advantage as a framework that can be adapted to the needs and the interests of the children that they work with, rather than regarding them as something that controls their practice. They were also adept in making the most of what they had in terms of their physical environment (e.g. not having a direct access to outdoors from indoor spaces), by working their way around these apparent 'constraints'. These practitioners exercised their autonomy in showing how they developed their own ways to create the best conditions for promoting the children's creative thinking.

The 'flow' of early childhood practice and teamwork

The ways in which practitioners exercise autonomy appear to facilitate the 'flow' of their practice. The concept of 'flow' has been described by Csikszentmihalyi (1990: xi) as one's 'total involvement' in one's life, in which the process is underpinned with joy and creativity (see Chapter 2). When applied to early childhood practice, this could be seen as practitioners' 'genuine enjoyment of being with children, and their total involvement in supporting their learning and development' (Fumoto, 2011: 28). One of the practitioners in the FRF project illustrates this:

When I'm working with small children I'm flowing, you know, I'm not really thinking about what I'm doing. It's reflexive. I'm responding and initiating and rethinking and returning and that's basically how I do it.

The experience of flow seems to show self-confidence on the part of the practitioners, which is associated with others' confidence in their professional judgement (Trotman, 2008).

Furthermore, shared values and expectations about children's learning and development seem to help a team of staff to maintain the flow of their practice. A shared sense of humour is important in dealing with stressful and difficult situations. As one of the practitioners commented:

> *I know this sounds funny but we tend to laugh ... There are days when we've just had enough but if you laugh your way through it then you can do it, you know ... and also I think it's really important, we all really, really, enjoy what we do and I think that plays a part as well, and because we get on as well.* (Cited in Robson and Fumoto, 2009: 50)

Professional commitment to knowing the children and their parents

Professional autonomy and the experience of flow are difficult to maintain without practitioners' commitment to knowing the children and their parents. The better practitioners know them, the more likely they are to see them in a different light, and this is important in developing communicative relationships with them. This is especially vital when practitioners work with children who demonstrate challenging behaviours. For instance, one of the teachers illustrates her relationship with a 5-year-old boy and the importance of her critical reflection on her own feeling towards him and on what he is trying to communicate with her:

> *At the beginning of the year ... I once had a child I didn't like. I don't know why, I really don't – there's nothing not to like – well there was. When it was time to clean up, he would hide. When he was asked to do something, he was just like [make a face] ... and now I look back to the notes that I made on him, the observational notes, and I have a page and a half when other children might have a third of a page. Every day, I was making notes about this boy to really see what was there and not what he was showing me. If you make your mind up that you're going to love that person, not in a huggy sweety way but really devote to what they need, you'll have a real affection for them and excitement about them growing ...* (cited in Fumoto, 2011: 24–5)

This reflection seems to stem from her willingness to 'stay open to new possibilities' and her awareness of the ways in which her practice influences children's learning and development. As she states:

> *So stay open, and expect a change in educator, and if you are still the same person you are 3 years from now, take a break.* (Cited in Fumoto, 2011: 26)

The pressing questions here are: how can practitioners deal with challenges in everyday practice if they fail to take the factors discussed in this section into account? How might this affect children and parents, and the practitioners' own well-being? In addition, Carr (2004: 61) suggests that the experience of flow in the context of work is observed more frequently in 'cultures that permit people to have work roles that are neither monotonously boring nor overly challenging and stressful, but where role demands meet workers' skill levels'. Does this mean that, for those who do not experience flow in their practice, there could be a mismatch between their levels of training and the demands placed upon them?

Conclusion

Practitioners strive to deal with various challenges that they experience in everyday practice in order to promote children's creative thinking. They bring important attributes to their practice that can help them deal with these challenges: in this chapter, they are identified as professional autonomy, the flow of early childhood practice, teamwork, and professional commitment to know the children and their parents. These factors, as DST indicates, are likely to shape their practice, and are therefore part of the developmental context of children. The ways in which these factors are, and should be, promoted depend on the local and cultural contexts of the settings. However, the practitioners in the FRF project and its related studies demonstrate the importance of their awareness of the impact that their practice can have on creating optimal conditions for children's effective learning and development, and indeed for the expression of their creative thinking.

The exploration of practitioners' experiences of promoting children's creative thinking leads us to consider several implications. The first concerns policy. As we have seen, the promotion of children's creative thinking is not a straightforward process: it is affected by many factors, including the challenges that practitioners face in their everyday practice. As they create conditions for children to extend their creative thinking, it should be stressed that practitioners also benefit from being in an environment that is conducive to doing so. Such an environment requires political commitment to enhance the resourcing of early childhood provision and the training of the workforce.

Secondly, there is the implication regarding professional development. Here, strong leadership and practitioners' determination to further improve their practice seem essential. As DST indicates, the attributes that practitioners bring to their practice can influence it to a considerable extent. As we have argued elsewhere, 'external factors by themselves do not determine the ways in which professionals make choices: it is the interaction between these factors and a professional's self-determination that shapes their practice' (Robson and Fumoto, 2009: 43). The professional commitment for them is to their continued engagement in upgrading their knowledge and skills in understanding children and parents.

Finally, there are some implications for research. Exploring practitioners' experience highlights challenges as well as the attributes they bring to their practice. The intention of this chapter has been to consider the promotion of children's creative thinking within the contexts in which practitioners work, since this process often seems detached from some of the wider factors that practitioners deal with in their day-to-day practice. A close examination of their experiences demonstrates a possible gap between theory and practice. We suggest that the 'communities of practice' approach to research (Chapter 7), which involves practitioners being part of the research community, is an important way forward.

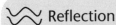 Reflection

- Consider the challenges identified in this chapter. How does each one look from practitioners', children's and parents' perspectives?
- How do the attributes that practitioners bring to their practice influence how they deal with the challenges identified in this chapter? Consider the kind of environment that would promote these factors in your own local and cultural context.
- Design and carry out a study that examines practitioners' experiences of promoting children's creative thinking.

11

Conclusions: towards understanding young children's creative thinking

Hiroko Fumoto, Sue Robson, Sue Greenfield and David J. Hargreaves

---

This chapter focuses on:

- The key issues that have emerged from considering children's creative thinking from children's, parents' and practitioners' perspectives;

- Implications for early childhood practice and theoretical and methodological approaches;

- Final thoughts on young children's creative thinking.

In the course of writing this book, it has been interesting to see that creative thinking has never left the news. In fact, there appears to be a sense of urgency in promoting children's creativity because of the uncertainty about what future society might hold. This is exemplified in the fierce public debate that occurs every time cases arise that seem to affect children's developing creativity. For instance, when Amy Chua, in her book *Battle Hymn of the Tiger Mother* (Chua, 2011), described how she raised her daughters in a parenting style that seemingly denied them any freedom to exercise their autonomy, it created much debate in the United States. The public debate concerned how children's creativity, and, indeed, their well-being may have been compromised. The issue of creativity was also hotly debated when the latest results of the OECD Programme for International

Student Assessment (PISA: OECD, 2009) was published. Many education-alists discussed how countries could develop education systems that would promote children's creative thinking and at the same time enhance their academic achievement. These public debates remind us how emotionally loaded issues such as parenting and pedagogy can be, and that the pro-motion of creative thinking is both a public and private concern. They have also made us reflect on our own view of parenting, and how we think about early childhood practice.

The aims of the book have been to look closely at the notion of creative thinking in an effort to bridge the gap in our understanding and to raise questions about how we might go about promoting it. In particular, we have critically evaluated the ways in which we engage children, parents and practitioners in research. In this final chapter, we reflect on some of the understanding that we have gained through our research and in writing this book, considering the implications for early childhood practice, and different theoretical and methodological approaches.

Social relationships in creative thinking: children, parents and early childhood practitioners

The common thread that runs throughout our discussion has been the importance of young children's social relationships at home and at school. The first part of the book provided the theoretical backgrounds to under-standing the links between social relationships and creative thinking, and discussed the social and cultural nature of creativity. Part 2 considered the ways in which we involve children, parents and practitioners in research, and highlighted the significance of developing collaborations with them within the spirit of 'communities of practice' (Denscombe, 2008). In the third part of the book, we examined closely the ways in which children express their creative thinking in early childhood settings, and how par-ents and practitioners promote it. As we have seen, promoting children's creative thinking is not a straightforward process. The prominent feature of our approach has been to understand children's creative thinking through the perspectives of children, parents and practitioners. Several key issues have emerged from this approach.

The first issue is the significance of ownership and autonomy experienced by children, parents and practitioners in their own learning, which is underpinned by the relationships that they develop with one another. As the title of the FRF project, *The Voice of the Child: Ownership and Autonomy in Early Learning* indicates, the importance of these two concepts in exam-ining children's experiences at home and at school has always been central to our investigations of the ways in which their creative thinking may be promoted. As we saw in Chapters 2 and 3, children's sense of ownership and autonomy in their activities is closely related to intrinsic motivation. They are thus likely to heighten the levels of *exploration, involvement and enjoyment*, and *persistence*: these are the behavioural categories that we identified in the *Analysing Children's Creative Thinking* (ACCT) Framework, developed for the project (Chapters 2, 3 and 8). Young children's involvement in activities could be initiated by themselves, adults or peers: its importance lies in the ways in which they take control of what they are doing (Chapter 8). This clearly demonstrates the significance of children's play in promoting their creative thinking, in which they can determine the course of their own actions.

The discussion in this book has also indicated the importance of ownership and autonomy in parenting and early childhood practice. As we have emphasized, concepts such as self-determination and self-efficacy are linked with one's sense of autonomy (Chapters 2, 3 and 10), and these are vital components in our lives and for our well-being. For early childhood practitioners, professional autonomy is also important in developing their own styles of practice and in finding ways of dealing with the challenges that they face in their everyday work (Chapter 10). Practitioners also play an important role in their support for parents in exercising their autonomy by developing trusting relationships with them. When we are constantly told what to do, be it by authorities, government, employers or by someone who is close to us, we begin to lose our confidence in dealing with them, and in having a sense of control over our lives. When this happens, we may become unable to maintain our psychological space to consider others' thoughts and emotions, as we are too busy trying to gain control over what we are doing ourselves. Parents and practitioners need this psychological space to listen sensitively to children's ideas and feelings, and to share the joys of discovering the world with them. Such moments may be essential in creating an environment that can promote children's creative thinking.

The second issue is the diversity of the expression of children's creative thinking. As we have discussed, our focus on home and school environments has led us to think about the multiple ways in which parents and practitioners develop relationships with children: a process which is embedded in their social and cultural contexts, and which is influenced by their personal attributes (Chapters 4, 6, 9 and 10). The ways in which parents and practitioners promote children's creativity can also vary, and, importantly, this process is mediated by the children's own perspectives. However, the diverse nature of children's creative thinking does not mean to say that there are no common elements: there are features of children's behaviour that we consider to be indicative of their creative thinking. These are outlined in the ACCT Framework, and provide a useful way of focusing our attention on children's ways of expressing their creative thinking (Chapters 3 and 9). What we do want to emphasize, however, are the diverse ways in which children express these common features. The idea of cultural contextualism (Kağıtçıbaşi, 2007) implies that it is important to extend the ways in which we consider children's creative thinking by moving away from a reliance on our own social and cultural perspectives (Chapter 4).

The third issue is how our understanding of children changes when we develop relationships with them. That is, once we get to know the children and have had the time to share some experiences with them, we are in a much better position to see their unique expressions of creative thinking. Practitioners' professional knowledge about the children is also significant for developing a deeper understanding of them. It is no wonder that parents and practitioners 'see' children in different ways, as they have very different relationships with them. Communication between parents and practitioners provides opportunities for sharing information about children which should help both of them to better understand the children, and to promote their creative thinking by listening to their thoughts more carefully.

The fourth issue is to understand creative thinking as a process and an ongoing aspect of children's development, rather than as a static factor in their lives. Over time, the ways in which children interact with and perceive their environment change, and so do the social relationships that they experience. In this book, our focus has been on their relationships with parents (primary caregivers) and with early childhood practitioners. But children's lives are influenced by a number of individuals around them. As Bronfenbrenner (1979) indicates, these all directly or indirectly contribute to children's development at different phases of their lives, with diverse impacts. Children's creative thinking is also likely to develop along with their evolving social and cultural contexts. What this implies is that we need to be open-minded about the different ways in which children might express their creative thinking. Some children who may not appear to be 'creative' could be quietly developing their creative thinking in their own ways. Indeed, what people are 'doing' may not always correspond with what they are 'thinking': we may be engaged in what appear to be 'uninspiring' activities, but what we are thinking may be completely different. As Watson (2011) writes, 'doing what you are told liberates the mind to think about something else. Those who suppose that routine is soul-destroying should try a little routine. A woman who knits is very unlikely to be thinking only about knitting'!

The fifth issue is the way in which social relationships can help channel children's creative energy. Whilst children's temperaments and the ways they perceive the environment can also affect the development of their creative thinking, the kinds of social relationships that they experience are likely to influence the ways in which they apply their creativity in society. This is thought to be especially important when we think about encouraging 'responsible forms of creativity' as opposed to 'unprincipled creativity' that lacks 'moral underpinning' (Craft et al., 2008c: 169–70). This does not mean to say that parents and practitioners are solely responsible for the ways children come to express their creativity. Indeed, social and cultural contexts could be only a part of the story of how children develop their creative thinking, albeit for us a very important part.

This fifth issue leads us to question just how much social relationships can influence the development of children's creative thinking. As Pinker (2002: 378) suggests, we may be 'misunderstand[ing] the effects of the genes' and overestimating 'the effects of the environment'. A theoretical framework such as developmental systems theory (DST: Ford and Lerner, 1992), discussed earlier in this book, presents a useful approach to understanding the interrelatedness between human nature and its environment. The ways in which we have emphasized the social and cultural nature of children's creative thinking (Chapter 4) also imply, to some extent, how some children may be more inclined to demonstrate those behavioural aspects identified in the ACCT Framework than others. This is an important question that needs to be kept in mind when we evaluate the effects that social and cultural contexts could have on children's development.

The final issue is the ways in which we place emphasis on the value of children's creative thinking in early childhood practice. Whilst we have made clear that not all of what young children do should be considered as an indication of their creative thinking, it seems important to consider some views that have been expressed about their creativity. Feldman, for example, cautions us against a 'romanticized' view of childhood and stresses that although many children are 'spontaneous, expressive, and unselfconscious in their willingness to say or do unconventional things', this should be distinguished from creativity that requires 'sustained focus, hard work, well-organized knowledge, persistence in the face of failure, and a coherent presentation of the work' (in Sawyer et al., 2003: 219–20). Moran suggests that: 'this folk belief about childhood creativity prevails because of our nostalgic view of childhood as a carefree time', adding that 'we underestimate children's generative abilities and so are more surprised when they say something original than if an adult says it' (in Sawyer et al., 2003: 224). Csikszentmihalyi asks: 'Why do people refuse to abandon the idea that the novelty of children represents creativity?' (cited in Sawyer et al., 2003: 223). These views and questions set important challenges when exploring young children's creative thinking.

One thing for certain, however, is that we want children to be happy and to be creative in ways that are meaningful to themselves and to the collective well-being of society. We believe that social relationships in early childhood play a significant role in shaping and extending children's creative thinking.

Implications for early childhood practice and theoretical and methodological approaches

Throughout the book, we have made many suggestions for early childhood practice, both within the text, in the case studies, and in the form of questions in 'Reflection' sections. As we have said, our aim was not to provide a 'quick fix' solution to practice. There are many ways in which professionals approach children's learning, applying their knowledge, skills and understanding to their unique situations, and any solutions to promoting children's creative thinking should be embedded in local contexts. We hope that our work provides opportunities for readers to reflect on the practical, theoretical and methodological issues presented in this book in relation to their own understanding of children's creative thinking. Here are some of the further implications that have arisen from our discussion:

- *To promote children's creative thinking means to enhance the quality of early childhood practice.* The more we look at children's creative thinking, the clearer it becomes that the promotion of creativity in young children is in line with 'high quality' early childhood practice. The ACCT can be a useful framework to guide practice, and we emphasize that effective communicative relationships between children, parents and practitioners should underpin this process.

- *In an effort to promote children's creative thinking, parents and practitioners should also nurture their own creativity.* If creativity is closely linked with self-esteem and well-being, it is also clearly important for adults. We should not lose our curiosity about the world. Parents and practitioners should explore it with children, as this can help to promote productive interaction with them.

- *The ways in which we promote children's creative thinking is an emotional topic which is strongly embedded in social and cultural contexts.* Often practitioners invest themselves in their work with children based on their own values of early childhood and children's learning and development. It is important to critically reflect on these, and see how they stand in relation to the children's and the parents' experiences of early childhood practice.

- *There should be stronger emphasis on the social and cultural aspects of children's creative thinking.* This is an important critical perspective on the study of children's creativity, and on the ways in which we interpret research findings, including both qualitative and quantitative approaches. It will also strengthen the critical examination of existing theoretical approaches to understanding children's creative thinking.

- *The need for further multidisciplinary and culturally diverse research teams.* Increasingly, efforts are being made to conduct research by groups of researchers with diverse interests and professional backgrounds. As this book has demonstrated, diversity can provide broader perspectives on an issue under investigation. Furthermore, the participation of children, parents and practitioners is essential when examining issues that concern young children.

- *Further exploration of creative thinking in the wider world.* We see evidence of creative thinking in our daily lives as well as in the news, reports and research from across the world. Exploring more critically the ways we see creative thinking around us could provide further insights into how people apply their creativity in their lives, and how it shapes society.

Final thoughts

It is important to note that conditions for parenting and early childhood practice do not exist in a vacuum. Supporting parents and practitioners to exercise their ownership and autonomy in ways that can support children's learning and development has significant policy implications. The ongoing focus on early childhood education and care by governments worldwide is encouraging, although the progress in terms of providing affordable high quality settings for all children sometimes seems painstakingly slow. Remuneration for the early childhood workforce continues to be generally low, making it difficult to always attract the most highly qualified staff. As has been discussed, these challenging circumstances could have serious implications for the development of the communicative relationships between children, parents and practitioners that are considered critical in promoting young children's creative thinking. We need political commitment to creating safe and secure environments in which good early childhood practice can thrive.

Further research on young children's creative thinking can also help promote not only our understanding of how children express their creativity, but also of parenting and early childhood pedagogy. We hope that issues discussed in this book have provided a basis for further development of the ways we explore children's creative thinking and their well-being at home and at school. In particular, our emphasis on the social and cultural nature of creative thinking should present important avenues for further cross-cultural research in investigating the diversity of parenting and early childhood practice, and the multiple ways in which children's creativity is being promoted across the globe.

References

Alasuutari, M. (2009) 'What is so funny about children? Laughter in parent–practitioner interaction', *International Journal of Early Years Education*, 17(2): 105–18.

Alderson, P. (2004) 'Ethics', in A. Fraser, V. Lewis, S. Ding, M. Kellett and C. Robinson (eds), *Doing Research with Children and Young People*. London: Sage. pp. 97–111.

Alderson, P. (2005) 'Designing ethical research with children', in A. Farrell (ed.), *Ethical Research with Children*. Maidenhead: Open University Press. pp. 27–36.

Alderson, P. (2008) 'Children as researchers: Participation rights and research methods', in P. Christensen and A. James (eds), *Research with Children: Perspectives and Practices*, 2nd edn. London: Routledge. pp. 276–90.

Alderson, P. and Morrow, V. (2004) *Ethics, Social Research and Consulting with Children and Young People*. Ilford: Barnardos.

Alexander, V.D., Thomas, H., Cronin, A., Fielding, J. and Moran-Ellis, J. (2008) 'Mixed methods', in N. Gilbert (ed.), *Researching Social Life*, 3rd edn. London: Sage. pp. 125–44.

Amabile, T.M. (1983) *The Social Psychology of Creativity*. New York: Springer Verlag.

Amabile, T.M. (1996) *Creativity in Context*. Boulder, CO: Westview Press.

Anning, A. (2010) '"Research" in early childhood settings: a pause for thought', *Early Years*, 30(2): 189–91.

Baldock, P. (2010) *Understanding Cultural Diversity in the Early Years*. London: Sage.

Ball, C. (1994) *Start Right: The Importance of Early Learning*. London: RSA.

Bandura, A. (1989) 'Human agency in social cognitive theory', *American Psychologist*, 44(9): 1175–84.

Banks, M. (2001) *Visual Methods in Social Research*. London: Sage.

Baum, A. and Swick, K. (2008) 'Dispositions towards families and family involvement: Supporting preservice teacher development', *Early Childhood Education Journal*, 35: 579–84.

Bergen, D. (2002) 'The role of pretend play in children's cognitive development', *Early Childhood Research and Practice*, 4(1), http://ecrp.uiuc.edu/v4n1/bergen.html (accessed 10 February 2005).

Bickham, D., Wright, J.C. and Huston, A.C. (2001) 'Attention, comprehension and the educational influences of television', in D.G. Singer and J.L. Singer (eds), *Handbook of Children and the Media*. Thousand Oaks, CA: Sage. pp. 101–19.

Boden, M.A. (1994) *Dimensions of Creativity*. Cambridge, MA: MIT Press.

Boden, M. (1999) 'Computer models of creativity', in R.J. Sternberg (ed.), *Handbook of Creativity*. Cambridge: Cambridge University Press. pp. 351–72.

139

Bourdieu, P. (1990) *Photography: A Middle-brow Art*. Cambridge: Polity Press.

Bradburn, E. (1967) 'Robert Owen – pioneer of nursery-infant education', *Froebel Journal*, 7: 22–5.

Brattico, E. and Tervaniemi. M. (2010) 'Creativity in musicians: Evidence from cognitive neuroscience', in R. Bader, C. Neuhaus and U. Morgenstern (eds), *Concepts, Experiments and Fieldwork: Studies in Systematic Musicology and Ethnomusicology*. Frankfurt: Peter Lang. pp. 233–44.

Bray, L. (2007) 'Developing an activity to aid informed assent when interviewing children and young people', *Journal of Research in Nursing*, 12: 447–57.

British Educational Research Association (BERA) (2004) *Revised Ethical Guidelines for Educational Research*. Southwell, UK: BERA, http://www.bera.ac.uk/files/2008/09/ethical.pdf

Broadhead, P. (2004) *Early Years Play and Learning*. London: RoutledgeFalmer.

Bronfenbrenner, U. (1979) *The Ecology of Human Development: Experiments by Nature and Design*. Cambridge, MA: Harvard University Press.

Bronfenbrenner, U. (2005) *Making Human Beings Human: Bioecological Perspectives on Human Development*. Thousand Oaks, CA: Sage.

Bronson, M. (2000) *Self-regulation in Early Childhood: Nature and Nurture*. New York: Guilford Press.

Brooker, L. (2002) *Starting School: Young Children Learning Cultures*. Buckingham: Open University Press.

Brooker, L., Rogers, S., Ellis, D., Hallet, E. and Roberts-Holmes, G. (2010) *Practitioners' Experiences of the Early Years Foundation Stage*. Research Report DFE-RR029. UK: Department for Education.

Brown, J.R., Knoche, L., Edwards, C. and Sheridan, S. (2009) 'Professional development to support parent engagement: A case study of early childhood practitioners', *Early Education and Development*, 20(3): 482–506.

Bruner, J. (1977) *The Process of Education* (revised edn.). Cambridge, MA: Harvard University Press.

Bryman, A. (2007) 'Barriers to integrating quantitative and qualitative research', *Journal of Mixed Methods Research*, 1(1): 8–22.

Buber, M. (1937) *I and Thou*. Trans. by R. Gregor-Smith. Reprinted in 1958. New York: Scribner.

Buchbinder, M., Longhofer, J., Barrett, T., Lawson, P. and Floersch, J. (2006) 'Ethnographic approaches to child care research', *Journal of Early Childhood Research*, 4(1): 45–63.

Burnard, P., Craft, A. and Cremin, T., with Duffy, B., Hanson, R., Keene, J., Haynes, L. and Burns, D. (2006) 'Documenting "possibility thinking": A journey of collaborative enquiry', *Early Years*, 14(3): 243–62.

Burnard, P., Cremin, T. and Craft, A. (2008) 'Introduction: What is creative learning?', in A. Craft, T. Cremin and P. Burnard (eds), *Creative Learning 3–11 and How We Document It*. Stoke-on-Trent: Trentham. pp. 1–2.

Buyse, E., Verschueren, K. and Doumen, S. (2011) 'Preschoolers' attachment to mother and risk for adjustment problems in kindergarten: Can takers make a difference?', *Social Development*, 20(1): 33–50.

Carr, A. (2004) *Positive Psychology: The Science of Happiness and Human Strengths*. Hove, UK and New York: Brunner-Routledge.

Chapman, C. (2006) 'Being a composer: The inside view', unpublished D.Psych. dissertation, City University, London.

Chen, Y. (2007) 'Equality and inequality of opportunity in education: Chinese emergent bilingual children in the English mainstream classroom', *Language, Culture and Curriculum*, 20(1): 36–50.

Christensen, P.H. (2004) 'Children's participation in ethnographic research: Issues of power and representation', *Children and Society*, 18: 165–76.

Christensen, P. and James, A. (eds) (2008) *Research with Children: Perspectives and Practices*, 2nd edn. London: Routledge.

Chua, A. (2011) *Battle Hymn of the Tiger Mother*. London: Bloomsbury.

Clark, A. and Moss, P. (2001) *Listening to Children: The Mosaic Approach*. London: National Children's Bureau and Joseph Rowntree Foundation.

Claxton, G. (1999) *Wise Up: The Challenge of Lifelong Learning*. London: Bloomsbury.

Claxton, G. (2006) 'Thinking at the edge: Developing soft creativity', *Cambridge Journal of Education*, 36(3): 351–62.

Claxton, G., Edwards, L. and Scale-Constantinou, V. (2006) 'Cultivating creative mentalities: A framework for education', *Thinking Skills and Creativity*, 1: 57–61.

Cohen, D. (2002) *How the Child's Mind Develops*. London: Routledge.

Coles, M.J. and Robinson, W.D. (1991) 'Teaching thinking: What is it? Is it possible?', in M.J. Coles and W.D. Robinson (eds) *Teaching Thinking: A Survey of Programmes in Education*. London: Bristol Classical Press. pp. 9–24.

Compton, A., Johnston, J., Nahmad-Williams, L. and Taylor, K. (2010) *Creative Development*. London: Continuum.

Connors, A.F. (2010) *Teaching Creativity: Supporting, Valuing and Inspiring Young Children's Creative Thinking*. Pittsburgh, PA: Whitmore.

Conroy, H. and Harcourt, D. (2009) 'Informed agreement to participate: Beginning the partnership with children in research', *Early Child Development and Care*, 179(2): 157–65.

Cook, N. (in press) 'Afterword: Beyond creativity?' in D.J. Hargreaves, R.A.R. MacDonald and D.E. Miell (eds), *Musical Imaginations*. Oxford: Oxford University Press.

Cousins, J. (1999) *Listening to Children Aged Four: Time is as Long as it Takes*. London: National Early Years Network.

Craft, A. (2001) 'Little c creativity', in A. Craft, B. Jeffrey and M. Liebling (eds), *Creativity in Education*. London: Continuum. pp. 45–61.

Craft, A. (2002) *Creativity and Early Years Education: A Lifewide Foundation*. London: Continuum.

Craft, A. (2003) 'Creative thinking in the early years of education', *Early Years*, 23(2): 143–54.

Craft, A. (2008) 'Creativity and early years settings', in A. Paige-Smith and A. Craft (ed.), *Developing Reflective Practice in the Early Years*. Open University Press. pp. 93–107.

Craft, A., Cremin, T. and Burnard, P. (eds) (2008a) *Creative Learning 3–11 and How We Document It*. Stoke-on-Trent: Trentham.

Craft, A., Cremin, T., Burnard, P. and Chappell, K. (2008b) 'Possibility thinking with children in England aged 3–7', in A. Craft, T. Cremin and P. Burnard (eds), *Creative Learning 3–11 and How We Document It*. Stoke-on-Trent: Trentham Books. pp. 65–73.

Craft, A., Gardner, H. and Claxton, G. (eds) (2008c) *Creativity, Wisdom and Trusteeship: Exploring the Role of Education*. Thousand Oaks, CA: Corwin Press.

Cremin, T., Burnard, P. and Craft, A. (2006) 'Pedagogy and possibility thinking in the early years', *Thinking Skills and Creativity*, 1: 108–19.

Creswell, J.W. (2009) 'Editorial: Mapping the field of mixed methods research', *Journal of Mixed Methods Research*, 3(2): 95–108.

Creswell, J.W. and Plano Clark, V. (2011) *Designing and Conducting Mixed Methods Research*, 2nd edn. Thousand Oaks, CA: Sage.

Crossley, N. (1996) *Intersubjectivity: The Fabric of Social Becoming*. London: Sage.

Crozier, G. (1999) 'Is it a case of "We know when we're not wanted"? The parents' perspective on teacher–parent relationships', *Educational Research Journal*, 41(3): 315–24.

Crozier, G. (2001) 'Excluded parents: the deracialisation of parental involvement', *Race Ethnicity and Education*, 4(4): 329–41.

Crozier, G. (2003) 'Researching black parents: Making sense of the roles of research and the researcher', *Journal of Qualitative Research*, 3(1): 79–94.

Csikszentmihalyi, M. (1990) *Flow: The Psychology of Optimal Experience*. New York and London: Harper Perennial.

Csikszentmihalyi, M. (1996) *Creativity: Flow and the Psychology of Discovery and Invention*. New York: HarperCollins.

Custodero, L.A. (2005) 'Observable indicators of flow experience: A developmental perspective of musical engagement in young children from infancy to school age', *Music Education Research*, 7(2): 185–209.

Custodero, L. (in press) 'The call to create: Flow experience in music learning and teaching', in D.J. Hargreaves, R.A.R. MacDonald and D.E. Miell (eds), *Musical Imaginations*. Oxford: Oxford University Press.

Dahlberg, G., Moss, P. and Pence, A. (2007) *Beyond Quality in Early Childhood Education and Care*. London: Routledge.

David, M., Edwards, R. and Alldred P. (2001) 'Children and school-based research: "Informed consent" or "educated consent"?', *British Educational Research Journal*, 27(3): 347–65.

Davis, H., Day, C. and Bidmead, C. (2002) *Working in Partnership with Parents: The Parent Adviser Model*. London: Harcourt Assessment.

Dawes, L., Mercer, N. and Wegerif, R. (2000) *Thinking Together*. Birmingham: Questions Publishing Company.

De Bono, E. (1968) *New Think: The Use of Lateral Thinking in the Generation of New Ideas*. New York: Basic Books.

de Boo, M. (1999) *Enquiring Children, Challenging Teaching*. Buckingham: Open University Press.

Deci, E.L. and Ryan, R.M. (eds) (2002) *Handbook of Self-Determination Research*. New York: University of Rochester Press.

Denscombe, M. (2008) 'Communities of practice: A research paradigm for the mixed methods approach', *Journal of Mixed Methods Research*, 2(3): 270–83.

Department for Children, Education, Lifelong Learning and Skills (Wales) (2008) *Framework for Children's Learning for 3- to 7-year-olds in Wales*. Cardiff: Department for Children, Education, Lifelong Learning and Skills.

Department for Children, Schools and Families (DCSF) (2008) *Practice Guidance for the Early Years Foundation Stage*. Nottingham: DCSF.

Department for Education (DfE) (2011) *The Early Years: Foundation for Life, Health and Learning*, http://media.education.gov.uk/MediaFiles/B/1/5/%7BB15EFF0D-A4DF-4294–93A1–1E1B88C13F68%7DTickell%20review.pdf (accessed 18 April, 2011).

Department for Education and Skills (DfES) (2007) *The Early Years Foundation Stage.* Nottingham, UK: DfES Publications.

Derksen, M. (2007) 'Cultivating human nature', *New Ideas in Psychology,* 25: 189–206.

Desforges, C. and Abouchar, A. (2003) *The Impact of Parental Involvement, Parental Support and Family Education on Pupil Achievements and Adjustment: A Literature Review.* Nottingham: DfES Publications.

Dietrich, A. (2007) 'Who's afraid of a cognitive neuroscience of creativity?', *Methods,* 42: 22–7.

Dockett, S. and Perry, B. (2005) 'Researching with children: Insights from the Starting School Research Project', *Early Child Development and Care,* 175(6): 507–21.

Dockett, S. and Perry, B. (2007) 'Trusting children's accounts in research', *Journal of Early Childhood Research,* 5(1): 47–63.

Donaldson, M. (1978) *Children's Minds.* Glasgow: Fontana/Collins.

Draper, L. and Wheeler, H. (2010) 'Working with parents', in G. Pugh and B. Duffy, *Contemporary Issues in the Early Years,* 5th edn. London: Sage. pp. 179–92.

Driessen, G., Smit, F. and Sleegers, P. (2005) 'Parental involvement and educational achievement', *British Educational Research Journal,* 31(4): 509–32.

Duffy, B. (2009) *Supporting Creativity and Imagination in the Early Years,* 2nd edn. Maidenhead, Berks: McGraw-Hill Education.

Dunn, J., Cheng, H., O'Connor, T.G. and Bridges, L. (2004) 'Children's perspectives on their relationships with their non-resident fathers: Influences, outcomes and implications', *Journal of Child Psychology and Psychiatry,* 45(3): 553–66.

Eckhoff, A. and Urbach, J. (2008) 'Understanding imaginative thinking during childhood: Sociocultural conceptions of creativity and imaginative thought', *Early Childhood Education Journal,* 36: 179–85.

Edwards, A., Sebba, J. and Rickinson, M. (2007) 'Working with users: Some implications for educational research', *British Educational Research Journal,* 33(5): 647–61.

Edwards, C., Gandini, L. and Forman, G. (eds) (1998) *The Hundred Languages of Children,* 2nd edn. Westport, CT: Ablex Publishing.

Edwards, S. (2007) 'From developmental-constructivism to socio-cultural theory and practice: An expansive analysis of teachers' professional learning in early childhood education', *Journal of Early Childhood Research,* 5(1): 83–106.

Einarsdottir, J. (2007) 'Research with children: methodological and ethical challenges', *European Early Childhood Education Research Journal,* 15(2): 197–211.

Eisner, E. (1985) *The Art of Educational Evaluation: A Personal View.* London: Falmer.

Family Policy Social Centre (2009) http://www.fpsc.or.uk (accessed 1 October 2011).

Fleer, M. (2003) 'Early childhood education as an evolving "community of practice" or as lived "social reproduction": Researching the "taken-for-granted"', *Contemporary Issues in Early Childhood,* 4(1): 64–79.

Fleer, M. (2006) 'The cultural construction of child development: Creating institutional and cultural intersubjectivity', *International Journal of Early Years Education,* 14(2): 127–40.

Fleer, M. (2008) 'The cultural construction of child development: Creating institutional and cultural intersubjectivity', in E. Wood (ed.), *Routledge Reader in*

Early Childhood Education. Abingdon: Routledge.

Fleer, M. and Robbins, J. (2007) 'A cultural-historical analysis of early childhood education: How do teachers appropriate new cultural tools?', *European Early Childhood Research Journal*, 15(1): 103–10.

Flewitt, R. (2005) 'Conducting research with young children: Some ethical considerations', *Early Child Development and Care*, 175(6): 553–65.

Flewitt, R. (2006) 'Using video to investigate preschool classroom interaction: Education research assumptions and methodological practices', *Visual Communication Journal*, 5: 25–50.

Ford, D.H. and Lerner, R.M. (1992) *Developmental Systems Theory: An Integrative Approach.* Newbury Park, CA: Sage.

Forman, G. (1999) 'Instant video revisiting: The video camera as a "tool of the mind" for young children', *Early Childhood Research and Practice*, 1(2), http://ecrp.uiuc.edu/v1n2/forman.html (accessed 20 June 2005).

Froebel, F. (1888) *The Education of Man.* Translated from the German by W.N. Hailmann, edited by K.J. Brehony, in facsimile of New York: Appleton & Company edition, 2001, London: Routledge.

Fumoto, H. (2005) 'Teachers' perceptions of teacher–child relationships in early childhood settings', unpublished PhD thesis, University of Surrey Roehampton, London.

Fumoto, H. (2011) 'Teacher–child relationships and early childhood practice', *Early Years*, 31(1): 19–30.

Fumoto, H. and Robson, S. (2006) 'Early childhood professionals' experience of time to facilitate children's thinking', *European Early Childhood Education Research Journal*, 14(2): 97–111.

Fumoto, H., Hargreaves, D.J. and Maxwell, S. (2003) 'Teachers' perceptions of teacher–child relationships in nursery schools', *European Early Childhood Education Research Journal*, 11(2): 29–42.

Fumoto, H., Hargreaves, D.J. and Maxwell, S. (2007) 'Teachers' perceptions of their relationships with children who speak English as an additional language in early childhood settings', *Journal of Early Childhood Research*, 5(2): 135–53.

Gallagher, M., Haywood, S.L., Jones, M.W. and Milne, S. (2010) 'Negotiating informed consent with children in school-based research: A critical review', *Children and Society*, 24(6): 471–82.

Gardner, H. (1993) *Creating Minds.* New York: Basic Books.

Getzels, J.W. and Jackson, P.W. (1962) *Creativity and Intelligence: Explorations with Gifted Students.* New York: Wiley.

Gibson, F. and Twycross, A. (2007) 'Children's participation in research: A position statement on behalf of the Royal College of Nursing's Research in Child Health (RiCH) Group and Children's and Young People's Rights and Ethics Group', *Paediatric Nursing*, 19(4): 14–17.

Glăveanu, V.P. (2010) 'Paradigms in the study of creativity: Introducing the perspective of cultural psychology', *New Ideas in Psychology*, 28: 79–93.

Gopnik, A. (2009) *The Philosophical Baby: What Children's Minds Tell Us About Truth, Love, and the Meaning of Life.* New York: Farra, Straus and Giroux.

Gorard, S. and Taylor, C. (2004) *Combining Methods in Educational and Social Research.* Maidenhead: Open University Press.

Greene, J.C. (2008) 'Is mixed methods social inquiry distinctive methodology?', *Journal of Mixed Methods Research*, 2(1): 7–22.

Greenfield, S. (2006) 'Will dyslexia unlock secrets of creativity?', *The Guardian*, Education section, 5 December 2006.

Greenfield, S. (2010a) 'The brain of the future: The impact of new technology on how we think and feel', invited talk at the London and Home Counties Branch of the British Psychological Society, London, 8 November.

Greenfield, S. (2010b) 'Working in multidisciplinary teams', in L. Miller and C. Cable, *Professionalisation, Leadership and Management*. London: Sage. pp. 77–90.

Greenfield, S. (2011) 'Nursery home visits: Rhetoric and realities', *Journal of Early Childhood Research*. DOI: 10.1177/1476718x11407983.

Grosse, G., Behne, T., Carpenter, M. and Tomasello, M. (2010) 'Infants communicate in order to be understood', *Developmental Psychology*, 46(6): 1710–22.

Guilford, J.P. (1950) 'Creativity', *American Psychologist*, 5: 444–54.

Hannon, P., Morgan, A. and Nutbrown, C. (2006) 'Parents' experiences of a family literacy programme', *Journal of Early Childhood Research*, 4(1) 19–44.

Hargreaves, D.J. and Bolton, N. (1972) 'Selecting creativity tests for use in research', *British Journal of Psychology*, 63: 451–62.

Hauari, H. and Hollingworth, K. (2009) *Understanding Fathering: Masculinity, Diversity and Change*. York: Joseph Rowntree Foundation.

Heath, S., Charles, V., Crow, G. and Wiles, R. (2007) 'Informed consent, gatekeepers and go-betweens: Negotiating consent in child- and youth-oriented institutions', *British Educational Research Journal*, 33: 403–17.

Hedegaard, M. (2009) 'Children's development from a cultural-historical approach: Children's activity in everyday local settings as foundation for their development', *Mind, Culture and Activity*, 16: 64–81.

Hennessey, B.A. (2003) 'The social psychology of creativity', *Scandinavian Journal of Educational Research*, 47(3): 253–71.

Her Majesty's Inspectorate of Education (HMIE) (Scotland) (2006) *Emerging Good Practice in Promoting Creativity*, http://www.hmie.gov.uk/documents/ publication/ Emerging%20Good%20practice%20in%20Promoting%20Creativity.pdf (accessed 27 April 2010).

Her Majesty's Stationery Office (HMSO) (1989) *Childhood Act 1989*. London, HMSO, http://www.legislation.gov.uk/ukpga/1989/41/contents (accessed 1 October 2010).

Her Majesty's Stationery Office (HMSO) (2004) *Children Act 2004*, http://www. legislation.gov.uk/ukpga/2004/31/pdfs/ukpga_20040031_en.pdf (accessed 1 September 2010).

Hill, M. (2005) 'Ethical considerations in researching children's experiences', in S. Green and D. Hogan (eds), *Researching Children's Experience: Methods and Approaches*. London: Sage. pp. 61–86.

Hill, S. and Nichols, S. (2009) 'Multiple pathways between home and school literacies', in A. Anning, J. Cullen and M. Fleer (eds), *Early Childhood Education: Society and Culture*. 2nd edn. London: Sage, pp. 169–84.

Hirsh-Pasek, K., Golinkoff, R.M., Berk, L.E. and Singer, D.G. (2009) *A Mandate for Playful Learning in Preschool: Presenting the Evidence*. New York: Oxford University Press.

Hobson, P. (2002) *The Cradle of Thought: Exploring the Origins of Thinking*. London: Macmillan.

Honig, A. (2001) 'How to promote creative thinking', *Early Childhood Today*, 15(5): 34–40.

Howes, C., Burchinal, M., Pianta, R.C., Bryant, D., Early, D., Clifford, R. and Barbarin, O. (2008) 'Ready to learn? Children's pre-academic achievement in pre-Kindergarten programs', *Early Childhood Research Quarterly*, 23: 27–50.

Hudson, L. (1966) *Contrary Imaginations*. Harmondsworth: Penguin.

Hutt, C. (1979) 'Exploration and play (#2)', in B. Sutton-Smith (ed.), *Play and Learning*. New York: Gardner Press. pp. 175–94.

Hutt, J., Tyler, S., Hutt, C. and Christopherson, H. (1989) *Play, Exploration and Learning: A Natural History of the Preschool*. London: Routledge.

James, A. and Prout, A. (eds) (1997) *Constructing and Reconstructing Childhood: Contemporary Issues in the Sociological Study of Childhood*. London: Falmer Press.

Johnson, R.B. and Onwuegbuzie, A.J. (2004) 'Mixed methods research: A research paradigm whose time has come', *Educational Researcher*, 33(7): 14–26.

Johnson-Laird, P.N. (1988) 'Freedom and constraint in creativity', in R.J. Sternberg (ed.), *The Nature of Creativity: Contemporary Psychological Perspectives*. Cambridge: Cambridge University Press. pp. 202–19.

Kağitçibaşi, Ç. (2007) *Family, Self, and Human Development Across Cultures*, 2nd edn. Mahwah, NJ: Lawrence Erlbaum Associates.

Katz, L. and Chard, S. (2000) Engaging Children's Minds. 2nd edn. Stamford, CT: Ablex Publishing.

Kaufman, J.C. and Beghetto, R.A. (2009) 'Beyond big and little: The four C model of creativity', *Review of General Psychology*, 13: 1–12.

Kaufman, J.C. and Sternberg, R.J. (eds) (2006) *The International Handbook of Creativity*. New York: Cambridge University Press.

Kaufman, J.C. and Sternberg, R.J. (2007) 'Resource review: Creativity', *Change*, 39: 55–8.

Kaufman, J.C. and Sternberg, R.J. (eds) (2010) *The Cambridge Handbook of Creativity*. New York: Cambridge University Press.

Kaufmann, G. (2003) 'What to measure? A new look at the concept of creativity', *Scandinavian Journal of Educational Research*, 47(3): 235–51.

Kellett, M. (2010) *Rethinking Children and Research*. London: Continuum.

Kemple, K.M. and Nissenberg, S.A. (2000) 'Nurturing creativity in early childhood education: Families are part of it', *Early Childhood Education Journal*, 28(1): 67–71.

Kenner, C., Ruby, M., Jessel, J., Gregory, E. and Arju, T. (2007) 'Intergenerational learning between children and grandparents in East London', *Journal of Early Childhood Research*, 5(3): 219–43.

Kim, K.H. (2005) 'Learning from each other: Creativity in East Asian and American Education', *Creativity Research Journal*, 17(4): 337–47.

Kim, K.H., Cramond, B. and Bandalos, D.L. (2006) 'The latent structure and measurement invariance of scores on the Torrance Tests of Creative Thinking-Figural', *Educational and Psychological Measurement*, 66(3): 459–77.

Knoblauch, H., Schnettler, B., Raab, J. and Soeffner, H-G. (eds) (2009) *Video Analysis: Methodology and Methods*. 2nd edn. Frankfurt am Main, Berlin, Bern, Brussels, New York, Oxford, Vienna: Peter Lang.

Knopf, H. and Swick, K. (2007) 'How parents feel about their child's teacher/school: Implications for early childhood professionals', *Early Childhood Education Journal*, 34(4): 291–6.

Knopf, H. and Swick, K. (2008) 'Using our understanding of families to strengthen family involvement', *Early Childhood Education Journal*, 35: 419–27.

Koberg, D. and Bagnall, J. (1991) *The Universal Traveler: A Soft Systems Guide to Creativity, Problem Solving and the Process of Reaching Goals*. Menlo Park, CA: Crisp Publications Inc.

Kochanska, G., Philibert, R.A. and Barry, R.A. (2009) 'Interplay of genes and early mother–child relationship in the development of self-regulation from toddler to preschool age', *Journal of Child Psychology and Psychiatry*, 50(11): 1331–8.

Kozbelt, A., Beghetto, R.A. and Runco. M. (2010) 'Theories of creativity', in J.C. Kaufman and R.J. Sternberg (eds), *The Cambridge Handbook of Creativity*. New York: Cambridge University Press. pp. 20–47.

Laevers, F. (2000) 'Forward to basics! Deep-level-learning and the experiential approach', *Early Years*, 20(2): 20–9.

Lahman, M.K.E. (2008) 'Always othered: Ethical research with children', *Journal of Early Childhood Research*, 6(3): 281–300.

Lahman, M.K.E. and Park, S. (2004) 'Understanding children from diverse cultures: Bridging perspectives of parents and teachers', *International Journal of Early Years Education*, 12(2): 131–42.

Lambert, E.B. (2000) 'Problem-solving in the first years of school', *Australian Journal of Early Childhood*, 25(3): 32–8.

Lave, J. and Wenger, E. (1991) *Situated Learning – Legitimate Peripheral Participation*. Cambridge: Cambridge University Press.

Lawson, M. (2003) 'School-family relations in context: Parent and teacher perceptions of parent involvement', *Urban Education*, 38(1): 77–133.

Learning and Teaching Scotland (2007) *Building the Curriculum 2: Active Learning in the Early Years*. Edinburgh: Scottish Government.

Learning and Teaching Scotland (2008) *Building the Curriculum 3: A Framework for Learning and Teaching*. Edinburgh: Scottish Government.

Lee, I-F. and Tseng, C-L. (2008) 'Cultural conflicts of the child-centered approach to early childhood education in Taiwan', *Early Years*, 28(2): 183–96.

Leontiev, D. (2006) 'Positive personality development: Approaches to personal autonomy', in M. Csikszentmihalyi and I.S. Csikszentmihalyi (eds), *A Life Worth Living: Contributions to Positive Psychology*. New York: Oxford University Press. pp. 49–61.

Lerner, R.M. (2002) *Concepts and Theories of Human Development*. 3rd edn. Mahwah, NJ: Lawrence Erlbaum Associates.

Levin-Rozalis, M. (2004) 'Re-visited: A tracer study 10 years later: detective process', *Journal of Early Childhood Research*, 2(3): 247–72.

Li, J., Yamamoto, Y., Luo, L., Batchelor, A.K. and Bresnahan, M. (2010) 'Why attend school? Chinese immigrant and European American Preschoolers' views and outcomes', *Developmental Psychology*, 46(6): 1637–50.

Liebschner, J. (1992) *A Child's Work: Freedom and Guidance in Froebel's Educational Theory and Practice*. Cambridge: The Lutterworth Press.

Lipman, M. (2003) *Thinking in Education*. Cambridge: Cambridge University Press.

Lipman, M., Sharp, A.M. and Oscanyan, F.S. (1980) *Philosophy in the Classroom*. Philadelphia: Temple University Press.

Lloyd, B. and Howe, N. (2003) 'Solitary play and convergent and divergent thinking skills in preschool children', *Early Childhood Research Quarterly*, 18: 22–41.

Lubart, T. (2010) 'Cross-cultural perspectives on creativity', in J.C. Kaufman and

R.J. Sternberg (eds), *The Cambridge Handbook of Creativity*. New York: Cambridge University Press. pp. 265–78.

MacNaughton, G. and Hughes, P. (2011) *Parents and Professionals in Early Childhood Settings*. Maidenhead: Open University Press.

MacNaughton, G., Hughes, P. and Smith, K. (2007) 'Young children's rights and public policy: Practices and possibilities for citizenship in the early years', *Children and Society*, 21: 458–69.

Malaguzzi, L. (1993) 'For an education based on relationships', *Young Children*, 49(1): 9–12.

Mandell, N. (1991) 'The least adult role in studying children', in F. Waksler (ed.), *Studying the Social Worlds of Children*. London: Falmer Press.

Martin, S. (2003) *Parents as Partners in Early Childhood Service in Ireland: An Exploratory Study*. Dublin: Dublin Institute of Technology.

Matsumoto, D. (2006) 'Culture and cultural worldview: Do verbal descriptions about culture reflect anything other than verbal descriptions of culture?', *Culture & Psychology*, 12(1): 33–62.

Mauthner, M. (1997) 'Methodological aspects of collecting data from children: Lessons from three research projects', *Children and Society*, 11: 16–28.

Mayall, B. (2008) 'Conversations with children: Working with generational issues', in P. Christensen and A. James (eds), *Research with Children: Perspectives and Practices*. 2nd edn. London: Routledge. pp. 109–24.

McGuinness, C. (1999) *From Thinking Skills to Thinking Classrooms*. Research Report 115. London: DfEE.

McMillan, M. (1930) *The Nursery School*. London and Toronto: J.M. Dent & Sons Ltd.

Meadows, S. (2006) *The Child as Thinker*. London: Routledge.

Melhuish, E. (2010) 'Why children, parents and home learning are important', in K. Sylva, E. Melhuish, P. Sammons, I. Siraj-Blatchford and B. Taggart (eds), *Early Childhood Matters: Evidence from the Effective Pre-school and Primary Education Project*. Abingdon: Routledge. pp. 44–69.

Mendez, J.L. (2010) 'How can parents get involved in preschool? Barriers and engagement in education by ethnic minority parents of children attending Head Start', *Cultural Diversity and Ethnic Minority Psychology*, 16(1): 26–36.

Mercer, N. (2000) *Words and Minds*. London: Routledge.

Merleau-Ponty, M. (1962) *Phenomenology of Perception*. (First English edition: trans. Smith, C.). London, New York: Routledge & Kegan Paul.

Miell, D.E. and Littleton, K. (eds) (2004) *Collaborative Creativity: Contemporary Perspectives*. London: Free Association Books.

Miller, E. and Almon, J. (2009) *Crisis in the Kindergarten: Why Children Need to Play in School*. Alliance for Childhood: College Park, MD, USA, http://www.allianceforchildhood.org/sites/allianceforchildhood.org/files/file/kindergarten_report.pdf (accessed 9 November 2009).

Miller, L. (2008) 'Developing professionalism within a regulatory framework in England: challenges and possibilities', *European Early Childhood Education Research Journal*, 16(2): 255–68.

Ministry of Education, New Zealand (1996) *Te Whāriki*. Wellington, NZ: Learning Media Limited.

Moloney, M. (2010) 'Unreasonable expectations: The dilemma for pedagogues in delivering policy objectives', *European Early Childhood Education Research Journal*, 18(2): 181–98.

Mondada, L. (2009) 'Video recording as the reflexive preservation and configuration of phenomenal features for analysis', in H. Knoblauch, B. Schnettler, J. Raab and H-G. Soeffner (eds), *Video Analysis: Methodology and Methods*. 2nd edn. Frankfurt am Main, Berlin, Bern, Brussels, New York, Oxford, Vienna: Peter Lang.

Morgan, A. (2007) 'Using video-stimulated recall to understand young children's perceptions of learning in classroom settings', *European Early Childhood Education Research Journal*, 15(2): 213–26.

Morgan, D.L. (2007) 'Paradigms lost and pragmatism regained: Methodological implications of combining qualitative and quantitative methods', *Journal of Mixed Methods Research*, 1(1): 48–76.

Morgan, W.J. and Guilherme, A. (2010) *'I and Thou:* The educational lessons of Martin Buber's dialogue with the conflicts of his times', *Educational Philosophy and Theory*, 1–18.

Morrow, G. and Malin, N. (2004) 'Parents and professionals working together: Turning rhetoric into reality', *Early Years*, 24(2): 163–77.

Morrow, V. and Richards, M. (1996) 'The ethics of social research with children: An overview', *Children and Society*, 10: 90–105.

Moyles, J., Adams, S. and Musgrove, A. (2002) *SPEEL: Study of Pedagogical Effectiveness in Early Learning*. London: DfES.

National Advisory Committee on Creative and Cultural Education (NACCCE) (1999) *All Our Futures: Creativity, Culture, and Education*. London: DfEE.

National Association for the Education of Young Children (NAEYC) (2009) *Developmentally Appropriate Practice in Early Childhood Programs Serving Children from Birth Through Age 8*. A Position Statement of the National Association for the Education of Young Children, http://www.naeyc.org/files/naeyc/file/positions/PSDAP.pdf (accessed 13 November 2009).

National Council for Curriculum and Assessment (NCCA) (Republic of Ireland) (2009) *Aistear: The Early Childhood Curriculum Framework*. Dublin: NCCA.

New, R.S. (2008) 'Rethinking research in early care and education: Joining Sally's quest', *Journal of Early Childhood Research*, 6(1): 59–67.

Nichols, S., Nixon, H., Pudney, V. and Jurvansuu, S. (2009) 'Parents resourcing children's early development and learning', *Early Years*, 29(2): 147–62.

Nisbett, R.E. (2003) *The Geography of Thought: How Asians and Westerners Think Differently – and Why*. London: Nicholas Brealey.

Office for Standards in Education, Children's Services and Skills (Ofsted) (2010) *Learning: Creative Approaches that Raise Standards*, www.ofsted.gov.uk/publications/080266 (accessed 20 April 2010).

Office of the High Commissioner for Human Rights (OHCHR) (2005) *General Comment No. 7 (2005: 01/11/2005). Implementing Child Rights in Early Childhood*, http://www2.ohchr.org/english/bodies/crc/comments.htm (accessed 13 July 2009).

O'Kane, C. (2008) 'The development of participatory techniques', in P. Christensen and A. James (eds), *Research with Children: Perspectives and Practices*, 2nd edn. London: Routledge. pp. 125–55.

Organisation for Economic Cooperation and Development (OECD) (2004) *Starting*

Strong: Curricula and Pedagogies in Early Childhood Education and Care. Paris: OECD.

Organisation for Economic Cooperation and Development (OECD) (2009) *OECD Programme for International Student Assessment (PISA)*, http://www.oecd.org/document/61/0,3746,en_32252351_32235731_46567613_1_1_1_1,00.html (accessed 11 April 2011).

Osborn, A.F. (1953) *Applied Imagination*, revised edn. New York: Scribner's.

Parke T. and Drury, R. (2000) 'Language development at home and school: Gains and losses in young bilinguals', *Early Years*, 21(2): 117–27.

Pascal, C. and Bertram, T. (2009) 'Listening to young citizens: The struggle to make real a participatory paradigm in research with young children', *European Early Childhood Education Research Journal*, 17(2): 249–62.

Penn, H. (2005) *Unequal Childhoods: Young Children's Lives in Poor Countries*. Abingdon: Routledge.

Peters, M., Seeds, K., Goldstein, A. and Coleman, N. (2007) *Parental Involvement in Children's Education*. London: Department for Children, Schools and Families.

Pianta, R.C. (1999) *Enhancing Relationships between Children and Teachers*. Washington, DC: American Psychological Association.

Pianta, R.C. (2001) *Student–Teacher Relationship Scale*. Lutz, FL: Psychological Assessment Resources, Inc.

Pike, A., Coldwell, J. and Dunn, J. (2005) 'Sibling relationships in early/middle childhood: Links with individual adjustment', *Journal of Family Psychology*, 19(4): 523–32.

Pink, S. (2007) *Doing Visual Ethnography*. 2nd edn. London: Sage.

Pinker, S. (2002) *The Blank Slate: The Modern Denial of Human Nature*. New York: Penguin.

Plowman, L. and Stephen, C. (2008) 'The big picture? Video and the representation of interaction', *British Educational Research Journal*, 34(4): 541–65.

Polydoratou, P. (2009) 'Experimenting with the trial of a research data audit: Some preliminary findings about data types, access to data and factors for long term preservation'. *ELPUB 2009: 13th International Conference on Electronic Publishing: Rethinking Electronic Publishing: Innovation in Communication* (Conference Proceedings). Italy: Nuova Cultura. pp. 291–307.

Pramling, I. (1988) 'Developing children's thinking about their own thinking', *British Journal of Educational Psychology*, 58: 266–78.

Prentice, R. (2000) 'Creativity: A reaffirmation of its place in early childhood education', *The Curriculum Journal*, 11(2): 145–58.

Project Zero/Reggio Children (2001) *Making Learning Visible: Children as Individual and Group Learners*. Reggio Emilia, Italy: Reggio Children Publications.

Pugh, G. and De'Ath, E. (1989) *Working Towards Partnership in the Early Years*. London: National Children's Bureau.

Qualifications and Curriculum Authority (QCA) (2005) *Creativity: Find It, Promote It*. London: QCA.

Qualifications and Curriculum Authority (QCA) (2008) *Early Years Foundation Stage Profile Handbook*. London: QCA.

Qualifications and Curriculum Authority/Department for Education and Employment (QCA/DfEE) (1999) *The National Curriculum Handbook for Primary Teachers in England*. London: QCA/DfEE.

Reedy, C.K. and McGrath, W.H. (2010) 'Can you hear me now? Staff–parent communication in child care centres', *Early Childhood Development and Care*, 180(3): 347–57.

Richards, R. (2006) 'Frank Barron and the study of creativity: A voice that lives on', *Journal of Humanistic Psychology*, 46(3): 352–70.

Richards, R. (2010) 'Everyday creativity: Process and way of life – four key issues', in J.C. Kaufman and R.J. Sternberg (eds), *The Cambridge Handbook of Creativity*. New York: Cambridge University Press. pp. 189–215.

Robson, S. (2006) *Developing Thinking and Understanding in Young Children*. London: Routledge.

Robson, S. (2009a) 'The physical environment', in L. Miller, C. Cable and G. Goodliff (eds), *Supporting Children's Learning in the Early Years*. London: Routledge. pp. 220–30.

Robson, S. (2009b) 'Producing and using video data in the early years: Ethical questions and practical consequences in research with young children', *Children and Society*, DOI: 10.1111/j.1099 0860.2009.00267.x.

Robson, S. (2010) 'Self-regulation and metacognition in young children's self-initiated play and reflective dialogue', *International Journal of Early Years Education*, 18(3): 227–41.

Robson, S. and Fumoto, H. (2009) 'Practitioners' experiences of personal ownership and autonomy in their support for young children's thinking', *Contemporary Issues in Early Childhood*, 10(1): 45–56.

Robson, S. and Hargreaves, D.J. (2005) 'What do early childhood practitioners think about young children's thinking?', *European Early Childhood Education Research Journal*, 13(1): 81–96.

Rogoff, B. (2003) *The Cultural Nature of Human Development*. Oxford and New York: Oxford University Press.

Rogoff, B., Turkanis, C.G. and Bartlett, L. (eds) (2001) *Learning Together: Children and Adults in a School Community*. New York: Oxford University Press.

Rose, G. (2001) *Visual Methodologies*. London: Sage.

Rothbaum, F., Pott, M., Azuma, H., Miyake, K. and Weisz, J. (2000) 'The development of close relationships in Japan and in the United States: Paths of symbiotic harmony and generative tension', *Child Development*, 71: 1121–42.

Runco, M.A. (2003) 'Education for creative potential', *Scandinavian Journal of Educational Research*, 47(3): 317–24.

Runco, M. (2007) *Creativity: Theories and Themes: Research, Development, and Practice*. New York: Academic Press.

Runco, M. A., Çayirdağ, N. and Acar, S. (2011) 'Quantitative research on creativity', in P. Thomson and J. Sefton-Green (eds), *Researching Creative Learning*. London: Routledge. pp. 153–71.

Runco, M.A. and Johnson, D.J. (2002) 'Parents' and teachers' implicit theories of children's creativity: A cross-cultural perspective', *Creativity Research Journal*, 14(3&4): 427–38.

Ryan, R.M and Deci, E.L. (2000) 'Self-determination theory and the facilitation of intrinsic motivation, social development, and well-being', *American Psychologist*, 55: 68–78.

Saft, E.W. and Pianta, R.C. (2001) 'Teachers' perceptions of their relationships with students: Effects of child age, gender, and ethnicity of teachers and children', *School Psychology Quarterly*, 16(2): 125–41.

Sammons, P., Sylva, K. Melhuish, E., Siraj-Blatchford, I., Taggart, B., Grabbe, Y. and Barreau, S. (2007) *Influences on Children's Attainment and Progress in Key Stage 2: Cognitive Outcomes in Year 5. Effective Pre-school and Primary Education 3–11 (EPPE 3–11)*. London: University of London, Institute of Education.

Samuelsson, I.P. and Pramling, N. (2009) 'Children's perspectives as "touch downs" in time: Assessing and developing children's understanding simultaneously', *Early Child Development and Care*, 179(2): 205–16.

Sarsani, M.R. (2008) 'Teachers' perceptions of creative learning in India', in A. Craft, T. Cremin and P. Burnard (eds), *Creative Learning 3–11 and How We Document It*. Stoke-on-Trent: Trentham Books. pp. 43–52.

Sawyer, R.K. (2003) *Group Creativity: Music, Theater, Collaboration*. Mahwah, NJ: Erlbaum.

Sawyer, R.K. (2010) 'Individual and group creativity', in J.C. Kaufman and R.J. Sternberg (eds), *The Cambridge Handbook of Creativity*. New York: Cambridge University Press. pp. 366–80.

Sawyer, R.K., John-Steiner, V., Moran, S., Steinberg, R.J., Feldman, D.H., Nakamura, J. and Csikszentmihalyi, M. (2003) *Creativity and Development*. New York: Oxford University Press.

Schiller, W. and Einarsdottir, J. (2009) 'Special issue: Listening to young children's voices in research – changing perspectives/changing relationships', *Early Child Development and Care*, 179(2): 125–30.

Seligman, M.E.P. and Csikszentmihalyi, M. (2000) 'Positive psychology: An introduction', *American Psychologist*, 55(1): 5–14.

Shears, J.K. (2007) 'Understanding differences in fathering activities across race and ethnicity', *Journal of Early Childhood Research*, 5(3): 245–51.

Shields, P. (2009) '"School doesn't feel as much of a partnership": Parents' perceptions of their children's transition from nursery school to reception class', *Early Years*, 29(3): 237–48.

Shin, M. (2010) 'Peeking at the relationship world of infant friends and caregivers', *Journal of Early Childhood Research*, 8(3): 294–302.

Simonton, D.K. (1990) 'History, chemistry, psychology, and genius: An intellectual autobiography of historiometry', in M.A. Runco and R.S. Albert (eds), *Theories of Creativity*. Newbury Park, CA: Sage. pp. 92–115.

Singer, J.L. (1973) *The Child's World of Make-Believe: Experimental Studies of Imaginative Play*. New York: Academic Press.

Siraj-Blatchford, I. (1993) *'Race', Gender and Education of Teachers*. Buckingham: Open University Press.

Siraj-Blatchford, I. (2007) 'Creativity, communication and collaboration: The identification of pedagogic progression in sustained shared thinking', *Asia-Pacific Journal of Research in Early Childhood Education*, 1(2): 3–23.

Siraj-Blatchford, I. (2010a) 'A focus on pedagogy: Case studies of effective practice', in K. Sylva, E. Melhuish, P. Sammons, I. Siraj-Blatchford and B. Taggart (eds), *Early Childhood Matters: Evidence from the Effective Pre-school and Primary Education Project*. Abingdon: Routledge. pp. 149–65.

Siraj-Blatchford, I. (2010b) 'Learning in the home and at school: how working class children "succeed against the odds"', *British Educational Research Journal*, 36(3): 463–82.

Siraj-Blatchford, I. and Manni, L. (2008) '"Would you like to tidy up now?" An analysis of adult questioning in English Foundation Stage', *Early Years*, 28(1): 5–22.

Siraj-Blatchford, I., Sylva, K., Muttock, S., Gilden, R. and Bell, D. (2002) *Researching Effective Pedagogy in the Early Years*. Research Report 356. London: DfES.

Smith, A., Duncan, J. and Marshall, K. (2005) 'Children's perspectives on their learning: Exploring methods', *Early Child Development and Care*, 175(6): 473–87.

Smith, P.K., Cowie, H. and Blades, M. (2003) *Understanding Children's Development*, 4th edn. Oxford: Blackwell.

Souto-Manning, M. and Swick, K. (2006) 'Teachers' beliefs about parent and family involvement: Rethinking our family involvement paradigm', *Early Childhood Education Journal*, 34(2): 187–93.

Sternberg, R.J. (ed.) (1999) *Handbook of Creativity*. Cambridge: Cambridge University Press.

Sternberg, R.J. (2003) 'Creative thinking in the classroom', *Scandinavian Journal of Educational Research*, 47(3): 325–38.

Sternberg, R.J. (2008) 'Leadership as a basis for the education of our children', in A. Craft, H. Gardner and G. Claxton (eds), *Creativity, Wisdom and Trusteeship: Exploring the Role of Education*. Thousand Oaks, CA: Corwin Press. pp. 143–57.

Sternberg, R.J. and Lubart, T.I. (1999) 'The concept of creativity: Prospects and paradigms', in R.J. Sternberg (ed.), *Handbook of Creativity*. Cambridge: Cambridge University Press. pp. 3–15.

Storr, A. (1988) *Solitude*. London: HarperCollins.

Sutton-Smith, B. (ed.) (1979) *Play and Learning*. New York: Gardner Press.

Swick, K. (2007) 'Insights on caring for early childhood professionals and families', *Early Childhood Education Journal*, 35(2): 97–102.

Swick, K. and Williams, R. (2006) 'An analysis of Bronfenbrenner's bio-ecological perspective for early childhood educators: Implications for working with families experiencing stress', *Early Childhood Education Journal*, 33(5): 371–8.

Sylva, K., Bruner, J.S. and Genova, P. (1976) 'The role of play in the problem-solving of young children 3- to 5-years-of-age', in J.S. Bruner, A. Jolly and K. Sylva (eds), *Play: Its Role in Development and Evolution*. Harmondsworth: Penguin. pp. 244–57.

Sylva, K., Melhuish, E., Sammons, P., Siraj-Blatchford, I. and Taggart, B. (2004) *The Effective Provision of Pre-School Education (EPPE) project: Final report – a longitudinal study funded by the DfES 1997–2004*. London: Institute of Education, University of London.

Sylva, K., Melhuish, E., Sammons, P., Siraj-Blatchford, I. and Taggart, B. (2010) *Early Childhood Matters: Evidence from the Effective Pre-school and Primary Education Project*. London: Routledge.

Sylva, K., Roy, C. and Painter, M. (1980) *Childwatching at Playgroup and Nursery School*. London: Grant McIntyre.

Tashakkori, A. and Creswell, J.W. (2007) 'Editorial: The new era of mixed methods', *Journal of Mixed Methods Research*, 1(1): 3–7.

Thinking Skills Review Group (2004) *Thinking Skills Approaches to Effective Teaching and Learning: What is the Evidence for Impact on Learners?* London: EPPI-Centre.

Thomson, P. (2008) *Doing Visual Research with Children and Young People*. London: Routledge.

Thomson, P. and Sefton-Green, J. (eds) (2011) *Researching Creative Learning*. London: Routledge.

Tovey, H. (2007) *Playing Outdoors*. Maidenhead: Open University Press.

Trickey, S. and Topping, K.J. (2004) '"Philosophy for children": A systematic review', *Research Papers in Education*, 19(3): 365–80.

Trotman, D. (2008) 'Liberating the wise educator: Cultivating professional judgment in educational practice', in A. Craft, H. Gardner and G. Claxton (eds), *Creativity, Wisdom and Trusteeship: Exploring the Role of Education*. Thousand Oaks, CA: Corwin Press. pp. 158–66.

United Nations (1989) *Convention on the Rights of the Child*, http://www2.ohchr.org/english/law/crc.htm

Urban, M. (2008) 'Dealing with uncertainty: Challenges and possibilities for the early childhood profession', *European Early Childhood Education Research Journal*, 16(2): 135–52.

Vecchi, V. (2010) *Art and Creativity in Reggio Emilia: Exploring the Role and Potential of Ateliers in Early Childhood Education*. Abingdon: Routledge.

Vincent, C. (1996) *Parents and Teachers: Power and Participation*. Abingdon: Routledge Falmer.

Vygotsky, L.S. (1978) *Mind in Society*. Cambridge, MA: Harvard University Press.

Vygotsky, L.S. (1986) *Thought and Language*. Cambridge, MA: MIT Press.

Vygotsky, L.S. (1991) 'Genesis of the higher mental functions' (abridged translation), in P. H. Light, S. Sheldon and M. Woodhead (eds), *Learning to Think*. London: Routledge and Open University Press. pp. 32–41. (Originally published 1966.)

Vygotsky, L.S. (2004) 'Imagination and creativity in childhood', *Journal of Russian and East European Psychology*, 42(1): 7–97.

Wallach, M. and Kogan, N. (1965) *Modes of Thinking in Young Children*. New York: Holt, Rinehart & Winston.

Wallas, G. (1926) *The Art of Thought*. London: Watts.

Watson, G. (2011) 'Heavenly task', *Times Higher Education*, http://www.timeshighereducation.co.uk/story.asp?storycode=414836&encCode=104056977BC64243875JTBS737226611 (accessed 11 April 2011).

Wegerif, R. (2010) *Mind Expanding*. Maidenhead: Open University Press.

Westerman, M.A. (2006) 'Quantitative research as an interpretive enterprise: The mostly unacknowledged role of interpretation in research efforts and suggestions for explicitly interpretive quantitative investigations', *New Ideas in Psychology*, 24: 189–211.

Whalley, M. and the Pen Green Centre Team (2007) *Involving Parents in their Children's Learning*. 2nd edn. London: Paul Chapman.

White, J. (2002) *The Child's Mind*. London: RoutledgeFalmer.

Whitebread, D. (2000a) 'Teaching children to think, reason, solve problems and be creative', in D. Whitebread (ed.), *The Psychology of Teaching and Learning in the Primary School*. London: RoutledgeFalmer. pp. 140–64.

Whitebread, D. (ed.) (2000b) *The Psychology of Teaching and Learning in the Primary School*. London: RoutledgeFalmer.

Whitebread, D., Anderson, H., Coltman, P., Page, C., Pasternak, D.P. and Mehta, S. (2005) 'Developing Independent Learning in the Early Years', *Education 3–13*, 33(1): 40–50.

Woodhead, M. and Faulkner, D. (2008) 'Subjects, objects or participants? Dilemmas of psychological research with children', in P. Christensen and A. James (eds), *Research with Children: Perspectives and Practices*, 2nd edn. London: Routledge. pp. 10–39.

Wright, S. (2010) *Understanding Creativity in Early Childhood*. London: Sage.

Index

DEVELOPMENTAL PSYCHOLOGY AND EARLY CHILDHOOD EDUCATION

A Guide for Students and Practitioners

David Whitebread *Cambridge University*

The importance of high quality early childhood education is now universally recognised, and this quality crucially depends upon the practitioners who work with our young children, and their deep understanding of how children develop and learn. This book makes a vital contribution to this understanding, providing authoritative reviews of key areas of research in developmental psychology, and demonstrating how these can inform practice in early years educational settings.

The book's major theme is the fundamental importance of young children developing as independent, self-regulating learners. It illustrates how good practice is based on four key principles which support and encourage this central aspect of development:

- secure attachment and emotional warmth
- feelings of control and agency
- cognitive challenge, adults supporting learning and children learning from one another
- articulation about learning, and opportunities for self-expression.

Each chapter includes:

- typical and significant questions which arise in practice related to that area of development
- an up-to-date review of key research, including insights from observational and experimental work with young children, from evolutionary psychology, and from neuroscientific studies of the developing brain
- practical exercises intended to deepen understanding and to inform practice
- questions for discussion
- recommended further reading.

CONTENTS

December 2011 • 184 pages
Cloth (978-1-4129-4712-1) • £60.00
Paper (978-1-4129-4713-8) • £19.99
Electronic (978-1-4462-5409-7) • £19.99

ALSO FROM SAGE